MANAGING GREEN ISSUES

Managing Green Issues

Tom Curtin

with Jacqueline Jones

St. Martin's Press, Scholarly and Reference Division,
175 Fifth Avenue, New York, N.Y. 10010

First published in the United States of America in 2000

This book is printed on paper suitable for recycling and made from
fully managed and sustained forest resources.

Printed in Great Britain

ISBN 0–312–23716–2

Library of Congress Cataloging-in-Publication Data

Curtin, Tom.
  Managing green issues / Tom Curtin.
    p. cm.
  Includes bibliographical references and index.
  ISBN 0–312–23716–2 (cloth)
  1. Environmental management. 2. Environmental responsibility.
  3. Social responsibility of business. I. Title.

GE300 .C78 2000
658.4'08—dc21   00–042078

For Nora, Tom, Sandra and Ray

Contents

Part IV
Communication Tools   **119**

List of Figures and Tables

Figures

Tables

Acknowledgements

We would like to thank many people – far too many to mention here – for their patience, help, advice and criticism. In no particular order and apologies to anyone left out – Harry Hudson, for his excellent proof reading, Cilla Everitt and Carla Bennett, Green Issues Communications, David Michie, Peter McIntosh, Sir Julian Oswald, Colin Duncan and Shirley Williams, Jayne Lake, Michelle Richards-Evans of Dacorum Borough Council, and, of course, Stephen Rutt of the publishers and Aardvark Editorial.

Part I
Introduction

1

Corporate Reputation in a 'Green' World

Today – some 40 years after the environmental movement started to become a real force in the world – most companies and large organisations still view it as a threat. They look at examples like Brent Spar and GM foods – not to mention something (once uncontroversial) like building a road or a house – and only see opposition. An opposition that seems to have the power to subvert the democratic will. Politicians seem powerless to act and, in some cases, seem to side with the green movement.

But where there is a threat, there is also opportunity. The world is now becoming dominated by brands. Companies that can deliver genuine environmental attributes and ethical qualities to their brands will have a huge advantage over those that cannot.

The threats

But managing reputation in an environmentally conscious world is not easy. Certainly, there is a need for direction and leadership from top management; certainly, it needs to involve employees, but it is not something that can be done in one fell swoop by a simple template which can be laid over the company.

It requires what most companies have the greatest difficulty in delivering – flexibility. Not just flexibility in work practices, which is now common, or flexibility in responsibility (empowerment was the buzzword of the *last* decade), but flexibility in three important areas:

1. *The organisation's goals.* Is it hell-bent on a 100 per cent success or can it be flexible and work on the principle that 99 per cent of a good win is better than 100 per cent of a loss?

2. *How it achieves its goals.* Can it be flexible enough to change, to take inputs from outsiders, many of whom it may regard as little better than nuisances?

3. *Who it uses to help it achieve these goals.* Organisations – and in particular large corporations – often have a machismo which tends to make them shun help. This is foolish. In the world of controversial issues, third party advocates – those who can speak on your behalf – are not just powerful, they are essential. This is a key tenet of this book.

To counter the threats and take advantage of the opportunity that the environment brings also takes total attention to detail. Throughout this book, about half the examples are at the local community level. It is here that problems arise which quickly escalate into national crises.

It is at this local level that the first tarnishes can begin to appear on the corporate image which can quickly spread to ruin the whole. Would Brent Spar be the issue it was had Shell not been in such a hurry (for very good reasons) to dump it, or would the UK's Newbury bypass (badly needed) have been such an issue if some local people had not supported the tree-dwellers?

In the world of issues management, no detail is too small.

The opportunities

The classic example of a company with strong environmental credentials is the Body Shop, which – almost totally without advertising and through strong linkages into green issues – has built a powerful brand.

Even something as mundane as do-it-yourself has seen the value of this approach: the UK chain, B&Q, has spent ten years devising an ethical and environmental stance for its brand – and shouting loudly about it. Why? Because it will increase sales and profits. The company takes great pride in the action plans it has devised and implemented.

A successful brand name and image enhance the value of a product, boost public confidence in that product and consequently, boost sales and share prices.

Brand names are often more important than the actual product. Richard Branson's Virgin brand, for example, is synonymous with high quality and service and is well known throughout the Western world. The Virgin name has been applied to all manner of things, from a radio station and music megastores to an airline, soft drinks and a train company. Even the exceptionally poor performance of his railway line has not put major dents in this carefully burnished brand and amazingly, the brand has stood strong in the face of huge criticism. Other areas that share the brand name appear not to have shared the shame.

Virgin is a unique case – most brands can be devastated by a single piece of bad press. Brands can be ruined for a long time by what may, at first, seem to be a fairly routine problem.

So how do companies manage, protect and mature their reputation in a green world? Corporate reputation should be built up from the micro-level. To maintain a good reputation a company or group should always be prepared for incidents. It is about attention to detail – ensuring you can prove that what you say is true and being ready to admit when you are wrong. You should be aware of your weaknesses before anyone else and act on them. It is the minute detail that will be picked up by the press and, by implication, the public.

Conclusion

This book deals with how companies can successfully manage controversial projects that have an impact on the environment. If they are managed well, the organisation will enjoy the spin-off benefits of a strong corporate reputation, which has important and positive implications for the brand image.

Part II

The World of
Green Issues

2 The Rise of Environmental Consciousness and Conscience

Environmental consciousness is the hallmark of a prosperous society. It is a rich country's prerogative. Therefore, it is not surprising that the greatest levels of environmental consciousness are probably in California which – despite pockets of abject poverty – has one of the highest average incomes per capita in the world. In 1998, $10 million was spent airlifting one whale from an aquarium back to its natural environment. They even made a film about it.

Green means rich

In the Third World, this sort of money means something else – especially when one considers that there are 1,300,000,000 people in the world living on less than $1 a day, a world where there are 840,000,000 people malnourished and – unlike the whale – 100 million are homeless. The money would have also bought 3 million water taps for Tanzanians who have no running water.

It is also the sign of a reasonably content, well-nourished and nurtured society. About 50 years ago, Maslow defined man's hierarchy of needs which are represented in Figure 2.1.

At the bottom is survival and the meeting of physiological needs such as air, food, water and sex.

Next is safety and this is followed by the need to be loved and to have a sense of belonging. Next up the scale comes esteem needs – manifested in a desire for a high level of self-respect and a need to feel valued.

Finally, at the top of the tree, is self-actualisation – the need to be involved in something which is outside ourselves – something which is

9

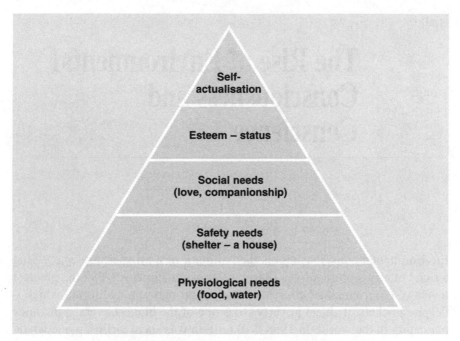

Figure 2.1   Maslow's hierarchy of needs reflects
today's environmental consciousness

precious and has almost a spiritual quality. The developed world today is
at the pinnacle of Maslow's hierarchy – even the reproductive urge is now
classed as recreational.

We feel secure and believe that we will survive, thrive and reproduce,
but a key concern is the environment in which we live. Not just our immediate environment, but the total planetary environment. This could be
defined as selfishness: we have enough; we have had our fill – no-one else
should have any more lest he damage it for us.

However, it not just selfishness – we also have a conscience about the
environment that we – in the developed world – have somehow not fully
paid for what we have taken from the planet; that we should not take any
more and, in many cases, give something back. So we buy cars that have
90 per cent recyclable parts. Whether they are ever recycled or not is
immaterial, we have done our bit to salve our conscience. After three
years, we trade them in and buy a new one.

Therefore it is not surprising that so many environmental campaigners
hark back to a different pre-technological age, a time before we had
despoiled the planet for our own benefit. The planet – our mother – gave

us all this: surely, we owe it to her to give something back – mainly by not taking any more?

However, this concern has knock-on effects. As all development – and, indeed, progress – will cause some environmental detriment there is a strong urge to preserve the world in aspic. This will mean that the rich will remain rich and the poor will remain poor and starving. There is a huge gulf opening up between the First and the Third World. The First World, for example, wants to save the tropical rain forests and dispatches its celebrities and others to champion it. Very laudable and, as we shall see throughout this book, the green groups have given a suitably emotional name to this campaign: to save 'the lungs of the planet'. No-one wants to lose their lungs and we can all relate to this.

But what the poor people who live in these regions want is survival – they are much lower down Maslow's scale. Not only do they want to survive, they want to climb the scale – even a little. They want money and the way to get it is to exploit their natural resources. After all, that is what the First World has been doing for the last half-millennium. And by a curious irony, this exploitation was not limited to the resources of Europe, North American and Japan: since the time of Columbus and da Gama, the developing world has been exploited by the First World. Now that they want to exploit their own resources the First World wants to stop them.

The Third World looks to the First and sees what development can bring. It pushes you up Maslow's hierarchy. And, they ask, why not? Certainly, the work of rain forest clearance is portrayed by the green groups as mighty multinationals imposing their will on the hapless natives. Not only is this view patronising, it is untrue. The local economies are willing and enthusiastic partners. They want the First World trappings: better health and education, to start with (2,000,000,000 have no electricity and one in five children does not attend primary school).

And how else can the poorer nations get better economic conditions, if not by their own development? The reluctance to cancel Third World debt is a sure indication that there are few handouts available.

Certainly, there are those naïve souls who would like to lock people of the Third World into a pre-technological age – citing their simple life-styles, how their culture will be lost and the stresses which modern Western civilisation induces. Besides being grossly patronising – it's too late. The genie is out of the bottle and will not go back. Like the lottery winners who say that their new-found wealth has brought them nothing but misery – the rest of us want to find out about this misery for ourselves. The people of the developing world want to try it for themselves. And who are we – with our Microsoft, Mercedes and McDonald's – to stop them?

However, the need of the First World to impose its environmental conscience on the Third can have more than adverse economic effects; it can be deadly.

SILENT SPRING – BUT WHO DIED?

One of the most evocative books on the environment was also one of the first: *Silent Spring* by Rachel Carson (1962). This examined the pesticide DDT and its detrimental effects on the food chain and the destruction of wildlife – hence the title. In many ways, this was also one of the key foundation stones which paved the way for the environmental movement – the industry as we know it today – to grow to its current size.

Following huge pressure by green or ecological groups, as they were known then, there was a public outcry, DDT was banned in the Western world, and replaced by more expensive alternatives. It was decided to stop its use throughout the world by the year 2007. Total effect on the developed world: a better environment all round.

But in the Third World, the results have been devastating. Malaria kills more than 2.5 million people per year – mostly very young children. It is also estimated that its debilitating effects mean that another 500 million – more than the total population of the USA – are in need of medical care and cannot work. The disease is transmitted by the mosquito.

Malaria has been eradicated in the Western world and it was also hoped that, like smallpox, it could be eradicated globally. The reverse is happening. The scourge of the West – DDT – has a vital role in fighting malaria in the developing world. When it is sprayed inside a dwelling, it either kills the mosquitoes or drives them away. However, with the pressure to reduce spraying of DDT, malaria is making a huge comeback. Surveys show that since DDT spraying was stopped in the mid-90s, the incidence of malaria in some countries has almost doubled.

There are alternatives, but they are not as effective. And they are all more expensive. Some green pressure groups claim that residues of DDT can be found in breast milk and that there are studies that link DDT use to cancer. However, there are far more studies that find no link.

Analysis

There is no doubt that the widespread use of DDT in the period after the Second World War was threatening major environmental damage. To curtail and ban its use was right – alternatives could be found. However, while there may be some doubts as to the safety of DDT in the Third World, there is no doubt at all about the lethal effects of malaria. Not just in the appalling toll on human life, but also on the economies of these countries with so many people debilitated by the disease. The question is: should First World ideology dictate survival in the Third?

So there is the dilemma: of course the environment should be protected, but at what cost? How many lives is it worth? If one were to look at the costs of environmental protection in global terms, and then to make decisions on how this money could be used to protect the greatest number of lives (again in global terms), it could be very difficult to justify some of the initiatives that the developed world has taken and is taking.

For example, the efforts to reduce carbon emissions are, for the most part, highly effective in the developed world, but in the developing world, they cannot be a priority. The priority here is survival and global warming – if it exists – is a problem for tomorrow. Still, we assuage our conscience by attempting to lower carbon emissions, blithely ignoring the fact that this is a global problem. Just because a few highly developed countries in the West meet their targets (while, by the way, the USA is ignoring them) will have little effect on what is a global problem if the rest of the world continues using fossil fuels at the rate the developed world did until recently.

A key economic indicator on our levels of environmental consciousness is how budgets of national governments have shifted. In the 1950s, the emphasis was on defence (survival), so there were huge budgets for the development of the atom bomb. There was no Environment Agency at that time. Today, the military machines of Europe are being dismantled, as Table 2.1 from NATO shows.

Today, the move is towards self-actualisation, to improving our external environment, and this is manifested in environmental protection. As expenditure on defence has fallen, expenditure on environmental protection has never been higher in the Western world.

Governments have set up huge departments whose role is environmental protection; most developed countries have environment agencies which act as watchdogs, and billions are spent on protecting the environment. Throughout Europe, billions of dollars are being spent to remove tiny harmless traces of pesticides from drinking water. Meanwhile in the Third World, drinking water is the source of most diseases and 2,600,000,000 have no access to sanitation – almost 40 per cent of the world's population.

The planet has never had it so good. And yet, there are high levels of concern, bordering on hyper-anxiety, about the environment that are at the top of most developed countries' agendas. For some, the green groups now sit at the cabinet table – the government formed by Schroeder in Germany in 1998 being the most obvious example. Their power is enormous, forcing giant multinationals like Shell to abandon plans to dump an oil platform – the Brent Spar – in the Atlantic, despite the encouragement of

| **Table 2.1** Defence expenditure as a percentage of gross domestic product (based on 1996 prices) | | | | | | | | |
Country	Average 1975–79	Average 1980–84	Average 1985–89	Average 1990–94	1992	1993	1994	1995	1996e
Belgium	3.2	3.3	2.9	2.0	1.9	1.8	1.7	1.7	1.6
Denmark	2.4	2.4	2.1	2.0	2.0	2.0	1.9	1.8	1.8
France	3.8	4.1	3.8	3.5	3.4	3.4	3.3	3.1	3.0
Germany	3.4	3.4	3.0	2.2	2.1	2.0	1.8	1.7	1.7
Greece	5.6	5.5	5.2	4.5	4.5	4.4	4.4	4.4	4.6
Italy	2.0	2.1	2.3	2.1	2.1	2.1	2.0	1.8	2.0
Luxembourg	0.9	1.1	1.0	0.9	1.0	0.9	0.9	0.8	0.8
Netherlands	3.1	3.1	2.9	2.4	2.5	2.3	2.1	2.0	2.0
Norway	2.9	2.7	2.9	2.8	3.0	2.7	2.8	2.4	2.5
Portugal	3.4	3.0	2.8	2.7	2.7	2.6	2.5	2.6	2.7
Spain	..	2.4	2.2	1.7	1.6	1.7	1.5	1.5	1.5
Turkey	4.4	4.0	3.3	3.8	3.9	3.9	4.1	4.0	4.4
UK	4.9	5.2	4.5	3.8	3.8	3.6	3.4	3.0	2.9
Nato Europe	..	**3.6**	**3.2**	**2.7**	**2.6**	**2.6**	**2.4**	**2.3**	**2.3**
Canada	1.9	2.1	2.1	1.9	1.9	1.9	1.8	1.6	1.5
US	5.0	5.8	6.3	4.9	5.1	4.8	4.3	4.0	3.7
North America	**4.7**	**5.4**	**5.9**	**4.7**	**4.9**	**4.5**	**4.1**	**3.8**	**3.6**
Nato total	..	**4.6**	**4.7**	**3.7**	**3.7**	**3.6**	**3.3**	**3.0**	**2.9**

the government and a vast body of scientific opinion to do so. Our environmental conscience and consciousness have never been higher and continue to rise.

Nature and environmental damage

There are only two major forces which can cause environmental damage: nature (or, in the words of the American architect, Frank Lloyd Wright: 'I believe in God, only I spell it Nature') and mankind. Nature is, of course, rapidly forgiven for its sins. The earthquakes in Turkey and Japan, the hurricanes that batter the USA, the floods in Bangladesh and other calamities cause – as well as enormous human fatalities and suffering – environmental damage on a vast scale – more than man could ever contemplate.

Nature has wiped out whole civilisations. The implosion that destroyed the Greek island of Thira thousands of years ago also wiped out the highly sophisticated Minoan culture that thrived there. In addition, the ash from the implosion was, some scientists argue, the cause of some of the pestilences that are recorded in the Bible as having been visited on Egypt.

And, of course, nature also wiped out the dinosaur. Mankind was definitely not to blame here – we didn't exist. Imagine the outcry today when just one tiny sub-species is slightly threatened with the most minor disruption. Plans to build a new road at Newbury in the UK were halted while the courts decided how much disruption would be inflicted on a tiny snail, which inhabited the proposed route. Badgers – considered vermin 100 years ago – have now acquired a semi-deified status.

But nature is powerful: the seas erode the coastlines which they have altered dramatically over the millennia, far more than the efforts of intensive farming and the lack of coastal defences. Naturally sparked forest fires change whole landscapes, and violent storms wreak havoc on both countryside and wildlife.

Conclusion

Leaving aside the selfishness, which many hide behind as the mask of protecting the environment, almost everyone claims to have an environmental conscience. No doubt this is true. After all, at worst, it is fashionable.

This is particularly so among the middle classes, who recycle their wine bottles and their fashion magazines and attempt to compost their rubbish. At the same time, they have two children and probably 'need' two cars (one a gas-guzzling fecundity symbol 'people carrier', and the other in which they commute to work).

Secretly, we know that children are environmental time-bombs, that our two cars are causing damage, so we need to 'do our bit' for the planet. So, we can drive to the bottle bank with our empty wine bottles without even considering the contradiction in what we are doing.

No-one undertakes an environmental cost/benefit analysis of any of the actions they undertake as part of 'doing their bit' for the environment. For the bottle bank, the environmental benefits of the recycling may be negated by the car journey. It all depends how much you drink and how far you travel. In many cases, you would have been better off staying at home and putting the bottles in the bin for the local landfill tip. And there is no world-shortage of sand. But, this cannot be a consideration. If we do consider it, it is rationalised by: 'Oh, I had to go to the supermarket and do some other errands on the way.'

Through these single-issue initiatives we assuage our environmental conscience.

And we are happy to impose our views on those parts of the world where they may cause real human damage. The questions we should be asking are: Could Europe have recovered after the Second World War with the levels of environmental protection which are placed on industry today? Is it fair that a Third World exists, in which the average Bangladeshi will have to work for eight years to buy a computer that a First World American can buy in a month? How can they catch up?

The answer is not by hindering progress in the developed world: we must continue to move forward or else we risk falling into the next Dark Age. However, the developing world needs a special status to allow it to have the advantages the First World had as it grew in the last 100 years: this means environmental damage.

Of course, we are worried about the environment in the developed world: at the top of Maslow's hierarchy we have everything to lose. Naturally, all of this is irrational, but what would you expect? After all, we are only human.

3

What Makes a Green Issue?

If something is an issue, it means that it is difficult, controversial and will arouse opposition. There are thousands of organisations, companies and projects which will never fit into this category. However, the difficulty is in finding out which projects or industries will suddenly fall into this category. This world is fluid and moves very rapidly. What was not an issue yesterday may be one today. Whale hunting was as acceptable 50 years ago (even celebrated in the novel and film *Moby Dick*) as cattle rearing is today. And it is not inconceivable to see a time when animal husbandry will be outlawed.

Who leads the green agenda?

However, for most organisations its issues are right on its doorstep. They may be small in the global sense, but that does not make them any less real or important. Although the examples used in this chapter are, for the most part dealing with more global issues such as nuclear power, GM foods and the like, they raise the same issues as those faced by a company that wants to build an extension to its factory.

There are those who claim that all environmental issues are led by the green groups; that they have a secret list of what will be the next hot topic. Certainly, they may have, but most issues are latched onto by the green groups rather than invented by them. Brent Spar happened almost by accident as far as Greenpeace was concerned. They needed something to increase their visibility, but more importantly, to keep some of their old hard-line direct-action campaigners happy: Brent Spar was an unexpected godsend. So, too, was the management of Shell, which turned what might have been a harmless disposal into some of the most exciting TV footage for years. Disposal at sea was not high on Greenpeace's list. Certainly, waste minimisation was, but it was difficult to get the media really excited about that, but the manifestation that was to become Brent Spar was a stroke of luck.

In addition to making something an issue, there are always outside and, as yet, unknown and unconsidered forces. When the British Prime Minister, Harold Macmillan, was asked what could go wrong in politics, he replied: 'Events, dear boy, events.' There are always 'events' that can quickly make an issue out of something that looks relatively harmless.

Again, Brent Spar is an example, but the leak of a sensitive document (particularly if it is still in draft) can be the event that makes an issue. And environmental issues are not confined only to the world or international stage. Issues now inhabit every community in the developed world. People are now even fighting the right to shelter as they oppose the building of new houses, yet they live in houses themselves. Anecdotally, it has been observed that those who live in the newest houses are the most vociferous in their opposition to the building of more houses. This is often because, as towns expand outwards, the next field is now their backyard. These people often forget that just a few short years ago, the land on which their house was built was also a green field. Issues are always surrounded by huge levels of irrationality: the risks of getting mad cow disease from eating beef have been estimated as being similar to the dangers from smoking one cigarette in one's lifetime.

Environmental issues – some indicators

The prediction of which events will become issues is as difficult as the science of earthquake prediction. While there may indicators, it is not fool-proof. Therefore, hard and fast definitions are difficult. However, there are certain characteristics and indicators that surround all environmental issues. They should be:

- simple in concept
- scientifically complex
- data rich
- open to speculation
- crisis prone.

They should also, ideally, have 'sloganability'.

Simple in concept

The issue must be very simple and be capable of being defined as either black or white. This allows sides to be taken – particularly by the media. So for Brent Spar the issue of sea dumping was bad and recycling of the structure on land (as advocated by Greenpeace) was good. GM foods are bad – we don't know enough about them. Organic foods are good. Nuclear power is bad (even though almost all developed nations use it) as the waste cannot be disposed of. Wind farms are good – even though they are unsightly and make a terrible noise, and produce only minuscule amounts of electricity.

Scientifically complex

Paradoxically, the science surrounding the issue must be extremely complex and impenetrable to the ordinary person. This is essential, as otherwise, people would be able to make a reasonable decision on what is right and what is wrong. So the science surrounding the disposal of the Brent Spar was very complex – how many pollutants were on the rig and how much damage could they cause? Would the rig, as it sunk to the bottom of the North Atlantic, provide a haven for the sea creatures there? Or would it damage the ecology of the ocean floor? The learned professors were wheeled out and argued over the heads of the populace.

The issue of nuclear waste disposal raises scientific questions which are effectively unanswerable: How can you predict what will happen in 50,000 years, let alone a hundred? Every discipline, from chemistry to geology, from sociology to astrophysics, can be called in and no definitive answer can be found. So, if all the scientific questions cannot be answered, then nothing should be done, argue the green groups. If that is what happens, then they have won. However, the waste will not go away and there then remains the ethical question: Is it right to leave all the dangerous material lying around for our children and grandchildren to play with?

And at a local level, the simple act of building a road, a shop or a housing estate now throws up reams of statistics. Every major new development requires a traffic impact assessment, which are all but impenetrable except to the consultants who wrote them. In addition, these statistics are capable of interpretation in many ways.

Data rich

Corporations today make available more data about their environmental performance than their predecessors ever had to (or did). These are published by the various agencies and are available to the public. Even confidential information is not safe: leaks of sensitive information are now commonplace. One sure way to get a document noticed and read is to mark it 'confidential'.

Even before the Internet, we lived in a world that was rich with data. In the USA, the Freedom of Information Act means that almost all data are available to everyone. However, turning the data into information is very difficult and turning this information into useable knowledge is another order of magnitude again. This semi-apocryphal story illustrates the point.

However, whereas our journalist did not have the time, the expertise or the expense account to spend days searching for the information, there are those who do. The major environmental groups can spend months trawling

---

THE CRUISE MISSILE THAT NEVER WAS

Most journalists enjoy travel. Ideally, like most of the people who sit in business class, they prefer to travel at someone else's expense. In the 1980s, with the Cold War still in full swing, the USA based a number of its Cruise missiles, armed with nuclear warheads, in the UK.

An Irish journalist realised that these missiles would have to be transported from the UK and could pass over Ireland. What, he thought, if the plane had engine failure and the bomb landed on, say, Dublin. He approached his editor who asked how he would get the flight paths of the planes. The journalist said that in the USA, because of the Freedom of Information Act, the information should be available. A dubious editor duly signed off the trip to the States.

One Monday, the journalist turned up at the Pentagon. He was greeted most civilly and brought to the library – a huge building on numerous storeys filled with reports, filing cabinets and books. He explained his purpose.

The receptionist said that he was welcome to all the information that was available in the room and that he was sure that there were some data that might help him. With the words, 'There's the photocopier, there's the coffee machine... and, hey, good luck,' he left the room.

Five days later our journalist returned to Dublin without his story on Cruise missiles, but instead a great yarn about drug abuse among Irish students who were taking working summer holidays. (As we will see in Chapter 13, like the Canadian Mounties who must always get their man, the media must always get a story.)

Analysis
The simple moral of this story is that if you want to hide a needle, first build a haystack.

through data. These are then presented as 'a major leak of a secret report' from the organisation in order to increase its media saleability.

Of course, the problem with all data is that when you turn it into information, it can be construed in a number of ways. So, for example, in the late 1980s, it was thought that Alzheimer's disease might be linked to the intake of aluminium. There were numerous studies that seemed to indicate that this could be a causal factor.

The environmental groups were very quick to latch onto the fact that there were traces of aluminium in tap water. They then used this to claim that drinking tap water could lead to the disease. This was at the height of the unpopular privatisation of the water industry in the UK, and received substantial coverage. The result: bottled water companies rubbed their hands in glee as sales got a boost.

As it turned out, the link between aluminium and Alzheimer's is now thought to be extremely tenuous. And the amount of aluminium in tap water is not even comparable to the dose you might get from, say, wrapping your sandwiches in foil.

The point is that – in environmental issues – there is no truth, there are only data. From these data, one can manufacture, quite legitimately, information which can be accepted by people (like those who bought bottled water) as knowledge.

Knowledge is our *perception* of what the facts are. In reality, in dealing with environmental and similar issues, there is no reality – there are just perceptions. These perceptions are what people believe and must be taken into account in dealing with the public.

Open to speculation
Here we have to apply the law of the absolute, since there has to be some element of doubt – which is why scientifically complex and data-rich projects make ideal environmental issues. There is a corollary to the law which says: the more you know the less you know. So, as science advances and more complex instruments are developed that are capable of identifying the presence of even the most minuscule levels of a substance, the more difficult it becomes to proclaim anything safe. More and more, as science makes advances, it throws new light, but it also shows how imperfect our knowledge is. Hence, the law of the absolute. So to the question, 'Can you categorically assure me that drinking mineral water with tiny traces of Benzene will never ever harm me?', the categorical answer of 'no' is not available. The next best answer is not good enough for our First World, health-conscious populace. This has powerful implications and its use by the media will be dealt with in Chapter 13.

This, of course, allows almost everything to become an issue. Categorical assurances are really not available for anything.

Naturally, environmentalists love the law of the absolute. It means that there is danger inherent in everything, which they are happy to point out to anyone who will listen, including grateful media.

Crisis prone

As Henry Kissinger once said: 'Do not let an issue become a crisis.' Yet that is what usually happens. The crisis may not be dramatic. A scientific report, showing that the populations of certain whales were diminishing rapidly, led to the campaign to save them. The safety of ocean-going supertankers only became an issue after the crisis of the *Exxon Valdez* in Alaska in the 1980s. By then, the memory of the last disaster, the *Torrey*

THE DANGERS OF OVERCOATS

The US magazine *Science* published a spoof on the dangers of overcoats, which are a great source of traffic accidents, according to Dr Noitall, who explains his theory: 'The average person walks across the street at 6.7076 kms per hour. When weighed down with a 2kg overcoat, a man of 75 kgs walks at 6.5201 kms per hour... the added exposure to murderous vehicles can easily be calculated to result in thousands of deaths every year.'

But how can this result in deaths? Dr Noitall again: 'The added risk per person is minor, but three or four billion people (six now since the article was written) on the planet are exposed to big-wheeled automobiles, big-wheeled oxcarts, wildly careering rickshaws and out-of-control tricycles.'

Dr Noitall blames the overcoat manufacturers for this supposed carnage and has an excellent answer when challenged on his figures. Perhaps it is not 6.5202, but 6.5201. *Science* comments: 'That is one of the great secrets of the propaganda of scares. Once a scientist says "There might be a problem," some ambitious reporter will say scientists are seriously considering the problem. While scientists try to nail down the fourth decimal place... the regulatory agencies say: "Scientists say there isn't a risk, but the data are still not certain, so we should be conservative and ban the product pending a study that determines its exact risk."

And if the study shows that the risk at four decimal places is negligible, Dr Noitall has a further strategy. 'If they solve the problem to four decimal places, I just ask for five. If they say that's trivial, I say I am worried about lives, whereas my opponents care more about money than lives.'

Canyon, off the south coast of England in the 1960s, had been forgotten. Since then, the whole question of the safety of these vessels has been an environmental issue. As in the case of the *Braer* – a large tanker which ran aground in the Scottish Isles – the threat of the environmental damage these vessels can invoke makes them an issue. In the case of the *Braer*, there was no major spillage and almost no environmental damage. Yet the perception – generated by the media and the green groups – was that this was an ecological disaster.

Indeed, it could be argued that an issue is not an issue until it either becomes, or has been, a crisis. The nuclear industry is typical of one which went from being a motherhood cause – promising unlimited supplies of electricity which was too cheap to meter – to today where the likelihood of building new nuclear power stations in most Western European countries is almost zero. To become such as issue, the industry suffered a number of crises, from Three Mile Island to Chernobyl and the Windscale fire.

Sloganability
The issue must be capable of being summarised in a couple of short words. This is also the essence of good branding: BMW is 'The Ultimate Driving Machine', for Avis, 'We try harder', and so on. So the disposal of nuclear waste is: 'Out of sight, out of mind.' GM foods are 'Frankenstein foods'. Houses are 'covering the countryside in a sea of concrete'.

Slogans like this are very hard to argue with – generally because they have enough truth in them to make them credible. In addition, large organisations – even though they may be brilliant at marketing – are not good at responding to this type of attack. The law of the absolute gets in the way. So the nuclear industry cannot respond, on nuclear waste disposal, 'Safe for all time' (even though it did in the UK in the 1980s!) – only God can say that. Neither can the GM industry come back with 'Food as nature intended'. These slogans are very hard to counter.

The semantics of science are appalling compared to the semantics of marketing, which is what the green groups exploit. They – like the devil – always have the best tunes. There are 'radioactive dumps' and 'Frankenstein foods'. But is science much better at describing the same things: neither 'repository' nor 'genetically modified organisms' exactly trip off the tongue, and, to be frank, sound less palatable. For media, there is no choice: the words to be used are those that are most understandable (the charitable view) or those that shock most (the cynical view). When trying to explain controversial scientific advances in the mass media, unfortunately, those that generate the most understanding and shock most are usually the same word.

Internal factors

However, issues are not just generated from outside forces. In addition, there will be a number of internal indicators. Today, the pace of change within organisations has never been higher. By its very definition, change means that the established order is altered and what was once normal may now become an issue.

Even attempts to improve matters can lead to an issue arising where there was none before.

CLEANING UP A LEGACY

As one of the forerunners of both nuclear power and nuclear arms, the UK has a historical legacy of radioactive plant and materials that need to be cleaned up. Much of this is the responsibility of British Nuclear Fuels Ltd (BNFL). In order to effect the clean-up process, the company constructed – at enormous expense – a new plant to deal with the legacy.

The new plant was constructed and went into operation. However, as with any clean-up operation, there must be some residues and, in this case, one was an element called Technetium 99. With the full authorisation of the regulatory authorities, minute quantities of this were released into the sea suspended in water. The risks were – and are still – considered negligible.

But enter the law of the absolute – can you guarantee that this compound will never cause any damage to any person, plant or animal EVER? Of course not.

Technetium is a man-made compound with a very long half-life that can be taken up by shellfish and crustaceans. Tests showed that this was happening. Theoretically, if you ate enough lobster for long enough, you could get a significant dose of radioactivity. Of course, the same could be said of thousands of naturally occurring products: if you eat enough of a certain type of nut (which is slightly radioactive) it is far worse than eating the lobsters.

However, the Technetium created a new issue and involved a number of countries. The controversy – ably fuelled by the green groups – rumbles on to this day.

Analysis

Needless to say, BNFL got very little credit for attempting what was, in effect, a fairly major environmental clean-up programme. The intent of what you do in an issue is immaterial, it is the end result that matters.

Again, of course, all of the characteristics just outlined were present. It was simple: radioactivity is bad, scientifically complex (what the hell is Technetium?), data rich (the scientists can argue till the cows come home), crisis prone and has sloganability (it can be linked to nuclear weapons).

However, an issue may also arise when almost nothing changes. It is the public's perception of the same thing. It is almost like shaking a kaleidoscope – the elements remain the same, but the picture changes.

THE BUBBLE BURSTS

By far the best example was Perrier where the management consistently ignored data which showed that it had trace amounts of Benzene in its mineral water. These amounts were rising and still the management ignored the warnings. This is not unreasonable; anyone who has worked in a chemistry laboratory will be familiar with this compound which is a fundamental chemical tool.

However, familiarity by the scientists was not enough to reassure the hyper-health-conscious people in Europe and, particularly, the USA. After attempts to talk down the scare, millions of bottles of Perrier were withdrawn.

But worse was to follow: it appeared that the Benzene was coming from a gas, which, although originated at the same source as the water, was added in a separate process. Suddenly the brand image of Perrier as being a pure natural product was shattered. Now it had intervention by man – it was an industrial process. The US authorities insisted that the labelling be changed.

Perrier was damaged irreparably and now the company is part of the Nestlé Group which has worked hard and successfully to re-establish what was, after all, a reputable and sound brand.

Analysis
Still, the lesson is a salutary one: getting your issues management wrong means you are in a very weak position to control the crisis when it breaks. This is very serious – in the worst cases, like Perrier, you lose the company.

Preparation for issues management

In effect, this is what this book is about – how to prepare for and then manage environmental issues. As noted at the beginning, the basis of predicted issues is a very difficult one. However, just because it is difficult does not mean that it should not be attempted.

Table 3.1   The potential issue

The indicators	Key questions	Ratings (out of five)
Simple in concept	Can this be easily and quickly understood by a non-scientist?	
	Does it provide the potential for real danger – not just to humans but to animals and plants also?	
	Do those who oppose look simply like the 'good guys' or do you look like the 'bad guys', that is, you are profit-making?	
Scientifically complex	Is it possible for a mischievous scientist to misrepresent this issue totally?	
	Is there seemingly contradictory evidence?	
	Is it a new field or an old one under modification?	
Data rich	Is there a substantial body of legislation?	
	Are there a great many scientific and technical studies?	
	Has someone tried to repress any of these data?	
Open to speculation	Is it possible to claim that it might kill or badly hurt people, animals or plants – even if this risk is minuscule?	
	Is it impossible to give categorical assurances on safety?	
	Are there 'rent-a-quote professors' who will speak out against the issue?	
Crisis prone	Has the industry been hit before?	
	Is there a siege mentality in the organisation?	
	Is there a fear of media, politicians, and so on?	
Sloganability	Is there a simple slogan which summarises the argument? (If one exists, the probability is that the slogan will be returned to)	
	Is it photogenic? Can it be made so?	
	Can it involve children, animals or flora?	
Internal issues	Has there been a substantial HR-generated change programme (culture)?	
	Have processes changed?	
Total	Max: 100	

Table 3.1 does not attempt to provide a definitive system or methodology for identifying what might become environmental issues. Rather, it is more like an early alert system. Try it with one particular project or

aspect of your business or organisation. A rating system has been adopted with the following measures:

5   Yes or very high or very likely
4   Probably or high or likely
3   Average
2   Unlikely or low or unlikely
1   No or very low or very unlikely

75–100

Obviously those projects, industries or aspects of industries which score about 75 should definitely have both proper crisis management and issues management programmes in place. Indeed, it is highly likely that they have – as they have been targeted before. Industries such as waste disposal, nuclear and the chemicals industry as well, nowadays, as the oil industry will come into this category. However, if the rating is high and there is no history, then one should be prepared. This was the situation all industries were in before an issue arose.

50–75

Certainly, issues like this are less likely to become controversial. However, times change and change quickly. It was only 40 short years ago that the nuclear industry was being hailed as the saviour of the planet and that Perrier was the drink of choice in fashionable downtown Hollywood.

25–50

Risk of becoming an issue is much lower here. This is where cattle-rearing was before BSE. It looks harmless, it looks safe, but given the right circumstances, it can explode. Again, it was an internal factor – the feeding of sheep carcasses to herbivorous cattle – which saw a multi-billion pound industry collapse.

20–25

Only the purest of the pure of the environmental groups can achieve this score.

Another useful exercise is to put oneself on the other side of the fence. Assume you are the local action group, the pressure group or whatever, and predict how you would react.

Conclusion

While exercises like this are useful and can help concentrate minds, all organisations must assume that – sooner or later – they are going to face something which will become an issue. And almost always, they only realise it is an issue because it has become a crisis. And in any crisis the best that one can hope for is damage limitation.

Far better than trying to isolate certain events, topics or processes that may become issues, an organisation should work to make itself bomb proof. In their book *Managing Outside Pressure* (Wiley 1998), Winter and Steger of the International Institute for Management Development (Lausanne) give a methodological system for evaluating the likelihood of an issue becoming a crisis, both from the company's and the activist's point of view.

For most organisations, this means fairly radical change in the way they approach their communication programmes. In order to do this, most have to change dramatically .

Prediction is imprecise? Yes. But then so is the world. Those who subscribe to chaos theory are well suited to becoming issues managers whose motto might be:

Expect the unexpected and then be really prepared.

4 The Environmental Movement – Corporations for a New Millennium

Today, the environmental movement is a huge industry with turnover measured in billions of dollars. Although its proponents try to portray themselves as altruistic amateurs, nothing could be further from the truth. These are finely honed, well-financed and highly efficient publicity machines. Just ask Shell, Exxon or Monsanto.

The green corporations

Within this industry – as one would find in any economic segment – there is competition between the various environmental corporations. So, if you ask Friends of the Earth which organisation poses the greatest threat to them, they should answer Greenpeace. They seek the same members and so compete for funds.

The green groups, however, now know that their marketplace is big enough for there to be a piece of the action for everyone. There has therefore – either consciously or unconsciously – been a market segmentation exercise. So Greenpeace does whales, Friends of the Earth does windmills and the Worldwide Fund for Nature does furry animals.

However, while many people support the aims of these organisations, not all are members, so the green groups have ongoing marketing campaigns through the usual methods used by mainstream corporations: direct mail, press relations campaigns, advertising and the like. These are expensive to mount, but there are more and more of them, so the green groups, while decrying the modern communications industry, have little hesitation in using its methods and becoming reference standards in the industry.

The green groups try to play down their PR activities – which they prefer to call campaigning. And, although they are among the most effective publicists in the world, they seldom win awards. (Within the communications industry there are a vast number of awards in advertising, marketing and public relations areas. In fact, rare is the agency that is not 'award winning'.) No, that would give the game away. When Greenpeace was working closely with the Body Shop, it very quickly distanced itself when the campaign won an award.

Co-operation and competition between green groups

There is obvious competition between the green groups, but there is also co-operation. Of course it is a matter of concern for Friends of the Earth and Greenpeace that its membership is getting older. It is also a concern for newspaper proprietors that its readership may be dying off and therefore they need to attract younger, higher spending new readers.

But there is an even bigger concern for these groups. The newer, more direct action, groups like EarthFirst! will begin to leach members from them. Even though EarthFirst! claims not to be an organisation (having no membership structure), this is worrying for the older organisations as it will cost them members. Therefore, they still need a number of direct action campaigns like Brent Spar and rooting up trials of genetically modified crops.

Despite the competition, the green groups are far better than mainstream corporations at forming strategic alliances. They are willing to leave their differences behind and work together. Of course, companies have trade associations to represent them, but these are never as effective as direct co-operation on the ground. (See Chapter 9 for a discussion on trade associations.) For example, Shell bore the brunt of the communications programme on Brent Spar by itself. But Exxon were 50 per cent owners: where were they and why were they not helping out?

The green groups are particularly adept at forging strategic alliances. Even the eco-warriors in the trees during the Newbury bypass saga had the local middle-class ladies bringing them bowls of soup and telling the world's media what fine fellows they were. How much in common did these people have? Not much, but they all wanted to stop that road.

While EarthFirst! was not directly involved at Peacehaven in the southern UK, where plans to build 113 homes were overturned, EarthFirst! claims that local community leaders turned to them for advice on direct action protest and tactics.

These strategic alliances can be transient and they are often – as at Newbury – only focused on one topic. It is unlikely that the eco-warriors took afternoon tea with the ladies before work began on the bypass.

Democracy and the green groups

What is most interesting about the democratic system is how all-pervasive it is. Every organisation looks for a system which reflects the wishes of the majority, be it the sports club in a small village or the national parliament. The system certainly has its faults. In the UK, no government in modern times has ever got 50 per cent of the available votes. Yet in 1997, New Labour got two-thirds of the seats in parliament. Certainly, there are corrective measures – like proportional representation, widely used in Ireland and mainland Europe – but the basic principle remains: the system is flawed but it's the best we've got. In effect, it means that 50 per cent plus one person can tell the other 50 per cent minus one how things are going to be run. Democracy is a tough system, it does not encourage consensus.

It is also galling for those people who lose at the election. They will now have to wait a long time in order to have another opportunity to put their policies into effect. There are a number of green groups who do not have that sort of patience.

However, democracy is not just about numbers at an election. It is also about the debate in the run-up to that election. This allows the people to listen to arguments from the various sides and to make reasoned judgements. Snap elections (called with, say, five days' notice) are essentially undemocratic. The debate is as important as the election itself.

The green groups – as reasonably reflected by the Green Party – fare particularly badly in democratic elections, with the possible exception of Germany. Here, they became part of Schroeder's power-sharing government in 1998 and control a number of regional assemblies. The Green Party is also represented in the French cabinet. However, in most countries the Green vote is well below 5 per cent.

If you are a member of a green group, this is a particularly frustrating state of affairs. Therefore, it is hardly surprising that the green groups tend to take the democratic process – and the law – into their own hands.

The rights of minorities

It is not suggested for a moment that minorities – no matter how insignif-
icant – do not have a right to be heard. They do. But only within the frame-
work of a democratic society and its laws. The acts of Greenpeace on the
uprooting of trials of genetically modified plants in the UK were outside
the law.

This was justified by Greenpeace in an article by Valerie Grove in *The
Times*, 31.07.99:

> I am clear that what we did was not illegal. We were justified in removing this pollution...
> The paradox is that Greenpeace is only ever accused of being undemocratic when we
> represent the views of millions of people in a way which can't be ignored.

But they were not *elected* to represent these views. Equally, the
debating phase of the democratic process mentioned earlier, is the opportunity to influence the arguments. Greenpeace chose to ignore the law and
democracy.

Already the green groups have had significant victories. There is no
party which is 'anti' the environment in a Western democracy. Environmental consciousness among politicians has never been higher. In fact,
mainstream politicians go to great lengths to out-green each other.

Neither should there be any further curtailment on the right to protest –
always enshrined in a modern democracy. The only caveat is that
protest should be within the law, and, in particular, it should not cause wilful
damage to people or property – as was the case with the GM crops protest.

However, one would be foolish to assume that the debate is just about
the environment – it is about (what Henry Kissinger referred to as ' the
ultimate aphrodisiac') power. And the green groups would like power –
this is natural and normal. What is not right is how they, at times, seek to
go about it.

Politicians and the green groups

Politicians, outside the Green Parties, are also quick to associate themselves with environmental causes and a great many are members of
Friends of the Earth, Greenpeace, and so on. The environment is a motherhood cause and is fairly safe from attack.

Members of national parties in many countries are active members of
green groups. This in part explains why the Green Party never does particularly well. Someone else has stolen its clothes.

THE MOTHERHOOD CAUSE

For some 400 years, the Catholic and Protestant politicians of Northern Ireland have been at loggerheads. There is a huge level of mistrust and antagonism between them.

But there is one thing they are in total agreement on: BNFL's nuclear facility at Sellafield is almost directly opposite Northern Ireland. Without exception, every politician in the country would like to see Sellafield shut down. This rare show of unity is amazing.

Analysis

Ireland, both North and South, has no nuclear industry. Certainly it has coal burning for electricity generation, from a fairly dirty coal-burning plant at Moneypoint in the West which, given the prevailing winds, brings the pollution from the South into the North. And, of course, it has the burning of turf from peat bogs, which many might say is not environmentally friendly. In fact, the Republic of Ireland has the highest level of CO_2 emissions per capita of any European country.

But nuclear it has not. So there is no mileage in supporting an industry on which no-one is dependent. So politicians from all sides can decry it. It is a motherhood cause. Politicians love these 'no lose' issues. They can speak openly and freely without fear of disaffecting one single voter.

However, the green groups can wield influence even if they are not in power. Majorities, particularly in local councils, are always slim: it is a brave politician who decides he or she does not want the green vote, which in many ways is now the wine-bottle recycling vote.

Conclusion

The world today is not one of black and white or of rationality. Today's world is one of persuasive arguments – it is a world of marketing, a world where people do not buy just the necessities of life, they are sold the delicacies and luxuries. One of these is the environment. And the green groups do a particularly good job in marketing this product.

But for an organisation, life is not that simple. The persuasive arguments are almost always on the other side. Appealing to rationality – as Monsanto tried to do in the GM foods debate – is a total waste of time and counterproductive.

Part III

The Practical Management of Green Issues

5

Identifying and Segmenting Stakeholders

It is the buzzword of the late 20th and early 21st century – the stakeholder. Like all words with an environmental connotation (such as sustainability) that are subject to overuse, it is also subject to abuse.

Stakeholders – a definition for a green world

What is a stakeholder in an organisation? The simple broad definition is an individual or group who may be affected – either beneficially or detrimentally – by the activities of the organisation. Obvious stakeholders include: shareholders in a company, employees, communities living near the organisation's operations and the like.

But today the definition is much wider. Companies are very quick to accept that anyone who claims to be a stakeholder in their enterprise must be one. This is a very dangerous argument. Therefore, before going any further, it is important to perform some sort of market segmentation – as one would do in any communications exercise – in those who claim to be stakeholders. For example, are Greenpeace stakeholders in Shell? Are EarthFirst! stakeholders of the North American logging industry? Is the Soil Association, a UK organisation with the backing of the Prince of Wales, a stakeholder in Monsanto, the lead organisation in genetically modified organisms?

In order to accommodate Greenpeace, EarthFirst! and the Soil Association as stakeholders in the respective organisations, one must adopt a very broad definition of a stakeholder. This is: an entity either affected by the operations of another organisation or one which perceives itself as having an interest in the activities of that organisation for whatever reason.

This definition means that every organisation is potentially a stake-holder of every other organisation, and the same applies to individuals, so it is next to useless, yet it is the one which is most commonly used. It is also the back door by which the green groups can claim to be stake-holders in organisations to which they are vehemently opposed. So, for example, Greenpeace, which is completely and irrevocably committed to the end of nuclear power on this planet, can enter into a dialogue with the likes of British Nuclear Fuels (BNFL), who are totally and irrevo-cably committed to the furtherance of nuclear power. Under the umbrella of the London-based Environment Council they are seeking a consensus. Obviously, none is possible, but then both sides know this and a clever game is under way. For Greenpeace, its credibility is enhanced in that it has brought BNFL to the table. Also, it is obviously now a major player on the broader political front in that BNFL is willing to take it seriously.

For BNFL, it is seen to be willing to consult even with its most vocif-erous opponents. It has attempted to shake off its old image of arrogance (given to it by Greenpeace) and secrecy (also given to it by Greenpeace.) BNFL can say to governments: 'We are open and reasonable people – after all, we sit down with Greenpeace.'

So BNFL gains from including Greenpeace among its stakeholders – even though that organisation does not in any way fit the simple definition of a stakeholder given at the beginning of this chapter. Greenpeace is not affected – either beneficially or detrimentally – by the activities of BNFL. Greenpeace is a Liberian-based pressure group, which represents only itself. It is not democratically elected and is hugely secretive about its activities, in particular its finances.

So, given that an organisation, for its own purposes, may assent to the broadening of the definition of what constitutes a stakeholder, then the second definition just given is more appropriate: in other words we are stakeholders of each other – in mathematical terms, there is only the universal set.

Obviously then, there is a need to segment this set into something more manageable. If this is not done, all stakeholders will be treated the same. Or, often worse, the most vocal stakeholders will be the only ones that are heard. This, incidentally, is the case with the three companies already mentioned: noise equals power. This is hugely dangerous, as many others have already found to their cost.

Therefore, as an initial broad segmentation, it is fair to say that there are three broad categories of stakeholder (see Figure 5.1):

- Those who want the organisation or project to *succeed* for their own benefit: employees, customers, and so on.

- Those who want it to *fail* so that it no longer affects them, Greenpeace versus BNFL, for example.

- Those who really are not overly concerned with the arguments, but who will be affected nonetheless (always by far the vast majority). For example, 80 per cent of French electricity comes from nuclear sources, so every citizen is a stakeholder in the nuclear industry, yet almost none is concerned about it.

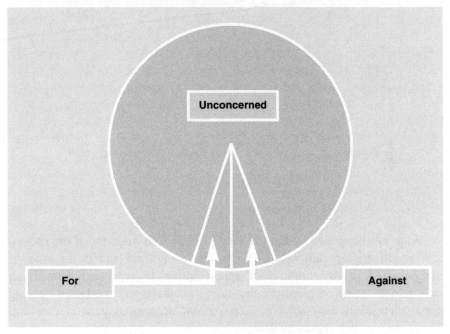

Figure 5.1   A quantitative view of stakeholders

For any project, Figure 5.1 is a fair representation of where the universe of people might stand. Even for the most controversial projects, a surprising number of people are essentially unconcerned. These three categories must be handled in very different ways and *not* equally. Unfortunately, what tends to happen is that the second category of stakeholders (those against) overshadows the real stakeholders, who are often among the unconcerned (see Figure 5.2).

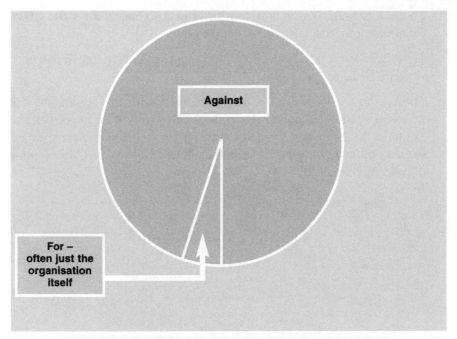

Figure 5.2　　Stakeholders are seen by the noise created

What has happened is that the views of the vast majority of the unconcerned citizens are not heard at all. This is normal and is the way of
democracy: it is why people elect representatives to 'represent' them. Even
in a modern large corporation, the chief executive and the board have to
make themselves accountable each year at an annual general meeting.
They, too, are just representatives.

But the green groups are, for the most part, unelected and, therefore,
unaccountable. The huge noise against projects such as Brent Spar and
GM foods are orchestrated and managed by just a few people. Certainly,
they are successful in changing public opinion on these issues, but that is
not a fault of the system. It is the fault of the company and it cannot shirk
this. Certainly, the media will play their part, but that is known and
expected. Politicians will play their part, but their behaviour, again, is both
known and predictable.

And yet – even though all of this is known – the vast majority of green
issues-related projects go wildly off course.

MONSANTO AND GREENPEACE

This is precisely what happened with Monsanto in the debate on genetically modified organisms. Greenpeace is vehemently opposed to the use of genetically modified organisms. In fact, so strong is its opposition that it does not believe that any research should be undertaken in this area. Although the research has the backing of governments, Greenpeace is not interested in the results: it has made up its mind that it wants no truck with GMOs. Full stop.

Monsanto is a leading company in this area. It ran a huge public relations and advertising campaign in an attempt to lay the facts in front of the people. This total campaign was based on a false premise. In *PR Week*, the UK public relations industry's weekly journal, Monsanto's PR agency, Good Relations, said it wanted to move the debate 'on to a rational footing.' The debate was lost as this point. Putting food for your children into a shopping basket is not a rational decision. It is an emotional decision and one where the vast majority of people – no matter how well educated on the facts and the rationality of the arguments – are not willing to take risks. To quote the old maxim of the experienced newspaper editor: 'When in doubt, leave it out.'

And doubt there was aplenty. Why? The only people speaking out for GMOs were all from Monsanto. Monsanto has a number of problems in Europe. First, it is American, and second, its chief executive was being paid the sort of telephone numbers that only US companies can manage. This perception – that they are only in it for the money – is very hard to shake.

Those speaking against Monsanto were a wide-ranging group. On a BBC 'Newsnight' programme, Monsanto put forward its spokespeople but Greenpeace was not to be seen. Instead, there were academics (independent, without doubt) and the chief executive of the frozen food retailer, Iceland. (The irony of a spokesperson for one form of food modification – freezing – speaking out against another form of modification was lost on the audience – and obviously on the BBC. And, of course, Iceland saw commercial advantage for itself in taking that stand.) The result was a total victory for Greenpeace, which was not even there!

So keen were Monsanto to show how fair they were being in the debate on GM foods that they actually printed Greenpeace's web address on the advertisements. So by doing this what were Monsanto saying to the world? Here are some thoughts:

- By far the most important stakeholder we have is Greenpeace, more important than our employees, our scientists, our customers, the politicians and regulators.
- In particular they are more important than the independent scientists who undertook much of the research work for us on GM foods; ignore these people and listen instead to Greenpeace.

> **MONSANTO AND GREENPEACE** *(cont'd)*
>
> The minute we convince Greenpeace that GM food is safe – and this won't be long! – they will endorse our stand.
>
> Even if these thoughts were not in the minds of the Monsanto communications experts – and no doubt they were not, even if they should have been – this is the strong perception which came across. Greenpeace was, of course, delighted and redoubled their efforts to stop even the testing.

Stakeholder segmentation

In classical marketing, one of the first exercises in any campaign is to segment the market. In a simplistic example, the sort of people who buy a Mercedes are probably different from those who buy a Fiat Uno – at least as their car for main use. Therefore, one needs to target messages to them in different ways and using different media. The Mercedes-buying business executive is influenced by different channels from the family looking for a small run-about. TV and radio stations, as well as print media, go to great lengths to show how effective they are at reaching specific audiences, by showing the percentage of various segments which can be reached through their outlets.

However, it is surprising that this simple exercise is seldom seen in mainstream public relations. One press release is written and sent to everyone. There is little effort to target within the media or fine-tune the message. And yet there is a great debate within the public relations industry as to why advertising budgets always outstrip those of PR and why the marketing effort is always led by advertising. The answer is simple: results.

As was seen with Monsanto and Greenpeace, the organisation which makes the most noise is seen as the most important and (often) the only stakeholder.

However, it is not difficult to apply a proper segmentation exercise to stakeholders. Earlier we already undertook the basic step of those who are 'for' the organisation and those who are 'against'. In the marketing of a car, this is comparable to those who are likely to buy and those who are not.

However, life is not so simple. Humans are complex creatures whose existence is nearly always a series of compromises. In controversial environmental projects, there are always shades of grey.

Here is a more complex segmentation where we have five different types of stakeholders:

1. *For the project*: totally committed.

2. *For – but with changes*: They are not against the project – they see the necessity for it, but they need to be convinced and certain doubts and concerns will have to be addressed.

3. *Neutral*: This is rare – decision-makers particularly will have some opinion. This may remain concealed – it should not be taken for neutrality. However, many people would remain unconcerned.

4. *Against with conditions*: Are they against but, with some modifications, might they begin to accept the proposal?

5. *Against*: Are they intractably opposed – they do not want the project, no matter what concessions are offered?

These can be mapped onto a diagram, as shown in Figure 5.3.

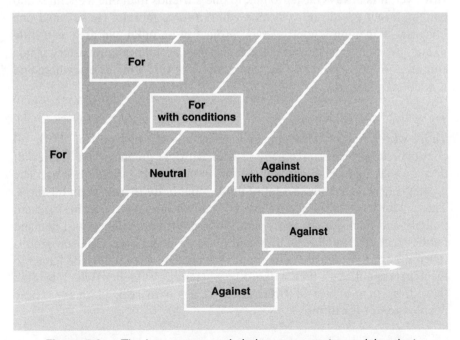

Figure 5.3   The key movers and shakers on a controversial project

This diagram is not to scale. If it were a diagram of the total population that is affected by a proposal, the unconcerned portion would be between 90–99 per cent, so they are not mapped here. They will take their lead from those who are active.

Unless people are directly affected by something they do not take an active stance: they do not attend public meetings, they do not write letters to newspapers, they do not lobby their politicians. When dealing with action or protest groups, we have found that nearly all decry the lack of activity in their fellow protesters: 'I am totally fed up,' said one, 'everything seems to fall to me and I have a full-time job and a family. There are only two or three of us who do anything.' The people on this diagram are active people: they may be affected by the proposals, they may be movers and shakers, the people who have decision-making power or who can influence those who have that power.

Let's look at each category in a little more detail.

Those totally for
Those who are 'totally for' are cosseted by the organisation. These people are usually in a tiny minority and are often seen as mavericks. They are not as useful as they seem – they are often seen as yes men or women. However, it is always easier to talk to one's friends than one's enemies and hanging around with the yes camp can reinforce morale. However, if one imagines managing a controversial project in an unknown area as a little like the work of missionaries, one is hanging around the monastery if one continues to concentrate on the yes camp. The real work is elsewhere and it is not as pleasant.

Those who totally oppose
Those who are intractably opposed are usually the first port of call in all controversial projects. 'We have to deal with the green groups – after all they are making a lot of noise about this issue,' is what is heard. Why? The green groups always make a lot of noise – publicity is their main business. Those who intractably oppose are not convertible. They are best treated politely and then, for the most part, ignored. Of course, they will demand public meetings (publicity), they will insist on being part of liaison groups (even though they are not democratically elected), they will write letters to the papers (publicity), they will produce scientific evidence (which is often flawed, as in the case of Brent Spar) – again to seek publicity. These people are not for turning.

The neutrals

These are rare, but their number is often exaggerated by those in a controversial project. 'Oh, Cllr Jameson has not spoken out on this, therefore he must be neutral.' Not necessarily: silence does not mean acquiescence. The councillor may be keeping his powder dry; he may be waiting to see how others are reacting; he may have strong views which he is going to use at a strategic time. Just because one does not know, do not presume neutrality.

Those with conditions

A closer look at the diagram shows something rather remarkable: there are not five categories; there are only four. Those 'who oppose with conditions' are the same as 'those who support with conditions'. In other words, if certain conditions are satisfied, then they will support the proposal.

However, too often those who oppose with conditions are consigned to the 'anti' camp. They are seen as the enemy. However, because they are not as vocal as the louder opposition, they are often ignored. Those who support with conditions are often treated the same way. Large organisations tend to think that they know best: after all, they have the engineers, the scientists, and have spent hundreds of thousands of pounds and many years researching this: what could well-meaning people on the ground possibly add to a project like this? The answer is, 'a successful outcome'. The following case illustrates the point that we have to be very careful in categorising our enemies.

THE TWO-HATTED TRADES UNIONIST

Trades unions were formed to look after the interests of their members, particularly in regard to wages and conditions of work. For many managers, they are seen as an unwelcome scourge. Certainly, when their powers become excessive, as happened in the UK during the 1970s, they can – like any single-issue pressure group – pose a real threat to democracy.

They can also be embarrassing to a company. In this case, the leader of a trades union was particularly vociferous when decrying the levels of boardroom pay, particularly that of the chairman, who in turn took all of this very personally. He deployed substantial resources in order to try to stop the trades unionist. In fact, he did everything except meet her.

THE TWO-HATTED TRADES UNIONIST *(cont'd)*

But the chairman's company was under threat from changes in impending government legislation, which could really damage the company's trading position and profitability. Naturally, the company employed professional lobbyists to put its case. Prime among their arguments were job losses, which they thought would appeal to the socialist government of the day.

However, time moved on and the lobbying firm was finding increasing resistance in its requests for meetings with key figures. The company was not getting its arguments across. Facing a desperate situation, a fairly junior public relations executive pointed out that the trades union – which had been such a thorn in the company's side – also sponsored a junior minister in the government department responsible for the new legislation.

'It's a waste of time,' said the lobbying firm, 'we have tried everything to get a meeting and it is impossible. It is probably because of the ongoing row about pay – he is too embarrassed to be seen to meet us because of the campaign run by his own union.'

'Why not,' suggested the PR executive, 'ask the trades unionist to go and meet him and explain the situation about job losses: particularly among her members.' This suggestion was greeted with horror.

There were two arguments against the suggestion: one overt and one covert.

The overt argument. The company would have no control over what she might say at this meeting. The simple answer to this is that it has no control over what she says in any event. So there is very little to lose.

The covert argument. But who would approach the trades unionist and ask her to approach the junior minister? In debate, the argument was hardly touched on. However, beneath the surface it had a huge influence. While the overt argument was debated again and again, the real fear – that of engaging an enemy – remained hidden.

As the situation became more desperate, it was decided to ask the junior PR executive to approach the union on the grounds that 'after all, it was your idea'. He called and, to his amazement, found a human being at the end of the phone who readily agreed to an informal meeting. It was the first non-confrontational contact she had had with the company for years.

The trades unionist was not aware of the magnitude of the problem and immediately saw the implications for her members. That week, she had secured a meeting with the junior minister and the senior minister and secured a change in the proposed legislation.

THE TWO-HATTED TRADES UNIONIST *(cont'd)*

Analysis

There are a number of lessons to be learned from this case.

1. We should never judge the book by the cover: often people are on the same side; they just don't know it.

2. It is very dangerous to generalise about people: just because they oppose one aspect of an organisation's activity does not mean they oppose it all.

3. The world is full of shades of grey – there is little that is black and white. This classification of 'you are either for us or against us' is very dangerous. Even members of political parties have different levels of commitment to their own party's policies and yet remain members of the grouping, as witnessed by the UK Conservatives' angst over membership of the Single European Currency.

4. When someone opposes a project – or, more importantly, is perceived to oppose it – we tend to have an almost paranoid fear about approaching them. They are the enemy: we cannot approach them, we must attack. This is a very dangerous strategy: it is only when one has a dialogue that the true agenda comes to the fore.

5. We all change our views with time. There is an old adage: 'He who is not a socialist at 20 has no heart, he who still is at 30 has no brain.' While the wisdom of the adage is open to question, it makes the point well.

Certainly, the trades unionist had conditions for her support for the company in this case: self-interest on behalf of the members of the union. And generally, people are best motivated when they are acting out of self-interest – it is a win–win project.

Yet, in the UK, many members of parliament are sponsored by trades unions, so obviously they still have power. Just because unions bargain hard for pay and better conditions does not necessarily make them opponents of the organisation. Employers often make the mistake of labelling the hard-nosed trades union negotiator as an intractable opponent, when, in fact, he or she may have unknown lobbying power. For another project which helps the company, he or she could become a powerful supporter.

The message from this exercise is simple. It is very rare to find 100 per cent agreement between two people, not to mention thousands across political barriers. Finding agreement means being willing to compromise. This is also very difficult.

Categorising stakeholders

After the crude segmentation exercise just encountered, it is possible to divide the stakeholders further into five main categories. (The unconcerned are not included as stakeholders as they do not want to be involved. If an individual or subgrouping does become involved, they will fall into one of the five other categories):

1. *Dependent stakeholders*: employees, suppliers, and so on
2. *Impacted stakeholders*: for example, those living near a facility
3. *Unknown stakeholders*: those who have not yet made themselves known
4. *Supporting stakeholders or third party advocates*: subsets of the previous three categories
5. *The intractables*: those who intractably opposed.

Dependent stakeholders

These are employees, suppliers and others who are, at least in part, dependent on the organisation's survival for their well-being. It is absolutely amazing that in times of crisis this group is almost totally ignored. Where were Shell's employees when the Brent Spar incident was at its height? Where were their trade unions? Where was the rest of the oil industry, in particular Exxon, a 50 per cent shareholder in the Brent Spar? If they did try to speak out, then their voices were not heard.

It is not surprising that when companies are under siege, they tend to 'circle the wagons'. This is a primeval instinct. When we are attacked we defend. However, to continue the allegory from the Wild West, there is nothing to stop an organisation calling the cavalry to come to its defence.

Dependent stakeholders can have a powerful voice. First, they are perceived to be independent. This is because, in perceptual terms, their self-interest is masked. So when a trade union – on behalf of employees – speaks out in favour of an organisation, what is perceived is:

- This is an independent organisation.
- It is fighting for jobs, always a good thing.

■ It is no-one's fool; in its watchdog role to protect employee rights, it has frequently attacked the company.

This form of third party advocacy, as we will examine in detail later, is very powerful. Dependent stakeholders are in a powerful position to become these advocates.

Impacted stakeholders

These stakeholders are not necessarily direct beneficiaries of an organisation's activities, but they are impacted by it: for example, some members of communities who live near a manufacturing plant, those who live near airports and are affected by noise, and so on. However, in many cases, they benefit directly, for example by the employment a manufacturing plant brings to a region, together with the other spin-off economic benefits.

THE GREEN ISLAND

One of the great examples of this type of stakeholding was the work of Ireland's Industrial Development Authority in luring US industry to set up manufacturing facilities in the country – in particular the pharmaceutical and electronics industries – from the early 1960s. Local communities – for years smitten by emigration – now had a source of jobs close to their homes. With some exceptions, these industries were, not unsurprisingly, welcomed with open arms as local people not only earned a living, but soon acquired new skills and eventually ended up running the plants. Of course, there was a downside in that, by its very definition, industry has an adverse environmental impact. However, it was not until the mid-1990s that signs of a backlash were beginning to be felt. And then it was isolated and localised.

However, too often impacted stakeholders are treated as enemies of the organisation. This is not necessarily so. Supposed opponents often disagree with just one small aspect of the project. Anyone who buys a house near an airport knows that there is going to be airport noise. Certainly, they may have convinced themselves (often because of price) that they can live with it, but now their objective is to improve the quality of their life. Naturally, they set about doing this by making demands on the airport authorities.

Near London's Heathrow airport, double-glazing was installed for residents to mitigate the noise impacts and this in some ways assuaged those who were opposed to further expansion of the airport. Of course, they are not suddenly going to drop their opposition to the expansion of the airport because double-glazing was installed, but the fact that both sides can agree on some mitigating measures helps lower the temperature and allows for a more constructive and positive dialogue.

It is also important to remember that groups are not necessarily representative of the totality of their community.

The unknown stakeholders

When we undertake these exercises in organisations, what always surprises the participants is the huge number of unknowns. 'To be honest, I don't think we know' is such a common response to many questions such as:

- Who else might be able to help you?
- What other organisations are in the same position as yourself?
- Who are the key individuals?
- Have they always been that way?
- What would be needed to change their minds?

An organisation can be compared to a balloon where everyone is on the inside looking out. The world looks concave. From the centre, the most important things are those which are nearest. Perceived enemies of the company have an uncanny ability to get under the skin of the organisation. This is particularly so in the case of a tetchy chief executive, who sees all forms of criticism as a personal affront which must be remedied immediately.

However, there is life outside the balloon and the perspective is convex. Things which look very damaging and important from the inside have little or no profile from the outside. And those outside the balloon have influence and can be hugely powerful with others. However, because they are outside the inner sanctum, they are seldom called upon. 'I am sure we have the resources in-house to handle this', comes the call from the chairman. The unknown forces remain, not just untapped – they are not even considered. No-one likes to be ignored, especially when he or she can contribute. Ask the university scientists who worked on genctically modified organisms.

This over-emphasis on internal resources leads the organisation to act, or in most cases, overreact. While it is easy to give perfect advice in hind-

sight, this is exactly what happened with Brent Spar. This lonely oil platform had no real profile until the water cannon started trying to dislodge
protesters in scenes which would have done justice to Hollywood. Of
course, Greenpeace was happy to video all of this – broadcast quality,
naturally – and release it to hapless and eager members of the media. The
ramifications for Shell are being felt to this day.

The supporting stakeholders or third party advocates

From the ranks of the dependent stakeholders, the impacted stakeholders
and the unknown stakeholders, comes the most important grouping of
stakeholders for a company. These are the supporting stakeholders, or third
party advocates as they are more commonly known. They are people who
are willing to defend the company's action and to do so publicly. They are
willing to take action.

Organisations are very slow to call on their support, mainly for some
of the reasons given earlier. However, if these reasons are examined carefully, in most cases it comes to little more than control mania. 'If we can't
control it, then we can't manage it', is one of the most dangerous management mantras there is. For this reason, large corporations (which are
particularly afflicted by this syndrome) brush aside those who might be
able to help them in times of danger.

The supporting stakeholders, or third party advocates, have a number
of characteristics:

1. *Selective support.* They do not support blindly all the organisation's
   actions. Corporations, particularly, are well equipped with people to
   do that – people whose jobs are dependent on obeying orders: the
   public relations department or press office. Often, third party advocates will only support the company on one particular project. They
   may oppose other projects: for example, a trades union official is
   likely to support a company's plans for expansion for one of its plants,
   but to oppose vociferously an internal re-organisation because it
   threatens jobs. The key thing to remember is the support, not the opposition, of this individual.

2. *Precedents are dangerous.* In the financial services industry customers
   are given a warning when taking out investments that past performance
   is not necessarily an indicator of the future. People change with time.
   Our opinions change, our prejudices change. As the former British
   Prime Minister, Harold Macmillan, said: 'When the facts change, I

change my mind, what do you do?' (These supporting stakeholders, or third party advocates, and how they act are examined in detail in Chapters 9 and 10.)

Intractables

Today, there are those – who claim to be stakeholders – whose only objective is to kill off the organisation of which they claim to be a stakeholder. Greenpeace and the nuclear industry or GM foods are typical examples. Under the guise of seeking consensus, these organisations' objective is to get close enough to kill off their prey.

Why consensus-seeking is useless

Consensus is only possible when both sides can reach some form of agreement on a final outcome. Consensus, in theory, allows one to be a little bit pregnant. So, one can have a little bit of nuclear reprocessing, but only on Tuesdays and Fridays; some GM foods are acceptable, but only in adult foods.

This is not consensus; this is the slippery slope to oblivion. The green groups are not foolish. They know that victory in a war is made up of a thousand battles. Each one that is won is another step to the ultimate victory.

THE END OF LEADED PETROL

In the early 1970s, a campaign was launched to phase out lead in petrol. The main reason was emerging evidence that the lead could damage children's brains.

At first, the campaign had little success, but given its high emotional content, that was soon to change.

The first step was to get the government to agree that lead in petrol was undesirable. The petrol industry reluctantly agreed with this and went on to fight about the levels of lead.

This was a huge and important victory for the anti-lead lobby. For the industry, it looked a success. Leaded petrol could continue, all that was needed was to reduce the levels. There was consensus.

THE END OF LEADED PETROL *(cont'd)*

However, as noted earlier, consensus is a slippery slope. With the new lower levels in place, the industry was content, the government was content and the public was reasonably content. Unleaded petrol was slightly dearer.

But the anti-lead lobby did not give up. The next step was to persuade governments to lower the price. Consumers who would not vote with their environmental conscience would surely vote with their pockets. The industry – which had already admitted that lower levels were acceptable – was in a very poor position now to fight against an incentive that would lower levels even further. The price reduction had a dramatic effect. Car manufacturers rushed to build new engines that would run on lead-free petrol. The result: today leaded petrol can not be found on the garage forecourt. Leaded petrol is banned throughout Europe. All from a move towards consensus in 1974.

Ironically, despite the fact that the governments of Europe have taken this unilateral decision, there is a still a strong debate on the merits of leaded versus unleaded petrol. Unleaded, for example, gives out high levels of Benzene, which has been associated with cancer.

As soon as one battle is won, green groups move immediately to the next. With GM foods, it was the insistence on labelling; when this victory was achieved, the next step was an outright ban.

Greenpeace first attacked the role of nuclear submarines, before turning its attention to the civilian industry that made them.

Although at first promoting consensus, the intractable stakeholders want you dead – out of business. Their only objective in consensus seeking is to get close enough to put the stake through the heart of your organisation.

Yet large corporations spend millions dealing with these troublesome people, while ignoring both the dependent and impacted stakeholders.

A new segmentation of stakeholders

From all this we can now produce a new way to segment the stakeholders and the would-be stakeholders in an organisation or project (see Figure 5.4).

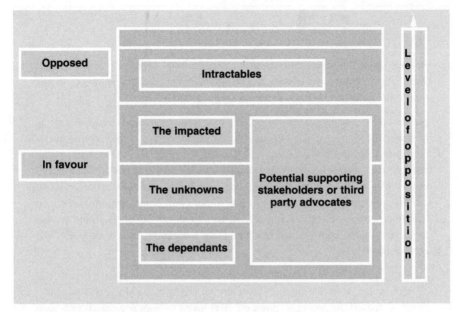

Figure 5.4   A new segmentation of stakeholders

Our new map of the stakeholders shows a number of interesting features. First, it is not just the dependants or stakeholders that can supply us with support. In fact, overdependancy can result in resentment. The employer who provides all ends up impoverishing its employees. Many will be resentful.

The unknown stakeholders provide a potentially richer ground for finding new supporters, as do the impacted stakeholders, who are often rejected because they show signs of opposition. However, these signs may only relate to one aspect of a project and it is vitally important not to generalise from one fact. Market research – a dangerous discipline in issues management – is even more unreliable if based on a sample of only one person, as is taking one incident as being representative of general views.

However, these people who might act as advocates for the company are useless if they do not take action.

Conclusion

It is too easy to assume that those who shout loudest are the most important stakeholders. This is not so. It is those who can help who should be given the most attention.

6

Stakeholders within the Power Pyramid

From the previous chapter, it is obvious that there are only a limited number of key stakeholders in any project. The vast majority of people remain unconcerned. However, before one can get involved in a project or a community, one must know something about the people with which one expects to deal. In any community – using the broadest definition of that word – the stranger is quickly spotted. Communities are now not just geographical entities – isolated from main centres. National parliaments form their own communities, so there is a community in Westminster, in Washington and in Brussels. It is where key players meet on familiar ground, where everyone knows everyone else and where the stranger is quickly spotted. The example used in this chapter is of a geographical community but the principle applies to communities of all sorts.

How democracy helps identify key stakeholders

In our search for the key stakeholders, we are greatly helped by the system of democracy to which almost all countries pay lip service, even if they do not actually manage to deliver. The democratic process based on universal suffrage is not as common as one might think. The UK, for example, fails the more stringent tests – with an unelected monarch and House of Lords.

A key tenet of this book is that democracy – although flawed – is preferable to all other systems of government. In the words of Sir Winston Churchill: 'Democracy's the worst form of government except for all the others.' This view does not suit everyone, as we saw in Chapter 4.

There are those who would seek to coerce the democratic will. And this is perfectly legitimate – even breaking the law is a legitimate action once, and only once, it is accepted that the law has been broken and that the proper punishments are meted out. Just because the law may change at some stage in the future does not make the present law invalid.

A further key tenet of democracy is freedom of speech and expression. The basic rule can be summarised as: 'I disagree totally with everything you say, but I defend totally your right to say it.' This is an aspect of the system that green groups are particularly adept at adopting for their own ends. And there is nothing at all wrong with this. However, what is good for a pressure group should also be good for the opposing forces.

The democratic system makes it fairly easy to find the first layer of key stakeholders. However, large organisations are not as fleet of foot as the green groups in getting to them: certainly, there are lobbying efforts but they tend to be fairly sterile: copperplate letters, newsletters, lunches with no agenda and the like. Large organisations are slow to approach people: they have some difficulty in getting really close to people – in essence, they are not good socialisers with those outside their close circle of friends and business. The hands-on common touch is replaced by the sterile corporate touch.

In addition, large organisations with disparate sites are usually remote from the areas in which they plan new projects. Often they are incomers to an area. By contrast, the green groups are particularly good at localising themselves. They even rebrand themselves: Cumbrians Opposed to a Radioactive Environment (CORE – the wittily named anti-nuclear group) is a bunch of activists funded (in the main) by Greenpeace. Friends of the Lake District (FOLD, another appropriate acronym in this sheep-rearing area) is the local chapter of the Council for the Protection of Rural England. And because they are local, and on the ground, they meet people and do it all the time.

An important principle of democracy is that the people elect representatives to speak on their behalf. This brings another definition of stakeholder – one who holds a stake on behalf of others. This is exactly what democracy is about. This is important and is recognised by politicians. And if the people do not like their politician stakeholders, they can get rid of them. Chris Mullin, Junior Minister in the UK's Department of the Environment, Transport and the Regions, said, when challenged on interference by politicians in planning at the annual conference of the Environmental Services Association in 1999: 'It is a principle of democracy that politicians can be removed when they are unpopular, and I am rather keen to cling on to it.'

However, our political system is complex. There are rules of protocol, for example. But more important, there is the need to find the right person to approach: there is little point talking to the chairman of the transport committee if your problem is to do with schools. Yet, this happens all too often. Before anyone is approached, it is important to know who he or she is, what he or she is, how he or she fits into the system and much more besides.

The power pyramid

In a democracy, power is not just concentrated at the top in the hands of the prime minister or president. Although, at times, it may look like that, power is fairly evenly distributed very differently from how it seems from the outside. Figure 6.1 shows how it could be represented from the outside.

However, this pyramid is the wrong way up – it is like a house built on its roof. In a democracy power flows from the bottom to the top and the power pyramid looks, in reality, more like Figure 6.2.

Certainly – as Figure 6.2 shows – a powerful leader will have considerable power, but like the iceberg, 90 per cent of the structure remains hidden. However, the tip of the iceberg cannot exist without the support of the 90 per cent. Also, there is a strong perceptual delineation between the

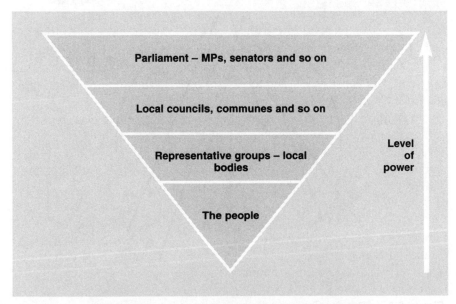

Figure 6.1 How the power structure in a modern democracy is often seen from the outside

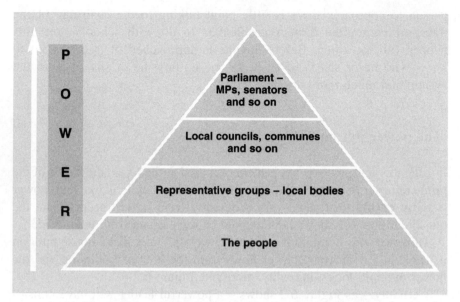

Figure 6.2   A simplistic version of the power pyramid

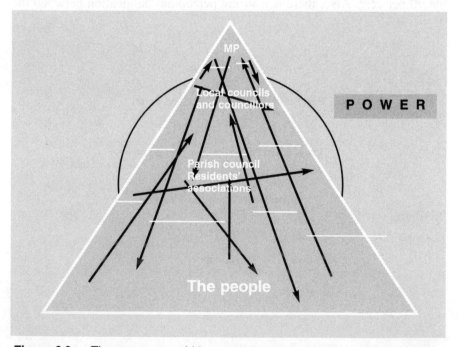

Figure 6.3   The power pyramid is a complex structure as this diagram shows. Power does not reside solely at the top – it is dissipated throughout the pyramid

various layers and levels of power. This does not reflect what actually happens. Figure 6.3 contains the power pyramid, which far more accurately reflects reality.

The power pyramid shows schematically a typical constituency that returns a member to the main national parliament. There are a number of important features in this figure:

- *Blurred lines of responsibility.* Unlike the earlier diagrams in the chapter, the lines of responsibility between the various layers merge and blur. There is no one point where responsibility or power stops. In the political system, there is freedom of movement. So, for example, a local resident can – and, indeed, will – approach his or her local parliamentary representative and put forward his or her views. And these views will be heeded.

- *Interplay between layers.* By far the most important feature is the level of interplay between the various layers, which gets more intense as one reaches the top. This is not surprising, as those at the top are often either professional or very dedicated politicians and so have more time to be active.

- *Apparent confusion.* Although this pyramid looks confused, unstructured and unregulated from the outside, it is not. It is governed by its own internal rules. And these rules vary from region to region and from council to council and from country to country.

- *The people factor.* Finally, one must not forget that this pyramid represents *real* people. And people are different in each different council, region or country. In one, there may be a powerful council leader and a relatively inexperienced MP – the interplay between these will be very different from when the reverse is true. In others, the grassroots – in terms of parish councils or residents' associations – may be powerful and in another, there may be none.

The level of complexity is not necessarily transparent to the outside observer. (In fact, it will often be denied by those within the pyramid.) Often the parliamentary representative seems to tower over his or her constituency. However, as the following case shows, a good representative is totally plugged into what is happening in every part of his or her constituency. That is why these politicians are often called representatives. They represent the views of those who elect them.

WHISPERING GRASSROOTS

A company wanted to locate a controversial waste incineration facility in a particularly densely populated area. After taking guidance from its lobbying firm, it decided to arrange a meeting with the local MP to 'sound her out'. The MP's secretary took the call from the lobbying firm. They explained that there was a potential major new development in her constituency and they would like to get views. An appointment was arranged between the chief executive of the waste company and the MP.

When the MP went through her diary with her secretary the next day, the appointment with the chief executive in four weeks' time was noted. The MP asked her secretary to be sure to make a note to raise the issue with her constituency chairman, who was also the leader of her political grouping on the local council.

A week later they met, and the constituency chairman said that any plans by a waste company would be strongly resisted. Something similar had been mooted some years ago and there was uproar. However, he would take some further soundings, particularly in the area that was considered last time. The MP naturally stressed the need for confidentiality at this time.

A week later, the MP reported back by telephone that there were still the remnants of an action group called FIRE (Firhaven Incinerator Resistance Effort). The local parish council and the residents' association would also no doubt be up in arms.

When the chief executive and the MP met the following week, she was very noncommittal, but stressed that there would be substantial opposition to the incinerator. The MP was a scientist by training and the chief executive was confident he could win her over by rational arguments about the safety precautions and the need for the facility. The chief executive outlined the technical reasons why the incinerator was needed, with numerous diagrams, pointing out how unobtrusive it would be and why her constituency was the best location. He also hinted there might a substantial package of 'goodies' on offer. She showed no interest in these.

Analysis

After all, 18 months before a general election in a marginal constituency, what other outcome could have been expected? The incinerator still has not been built.

Starting at the top of the power pyramid is a waste of time. It is rather like being helicoptered onto Mount Everest with the intention of walking down. It proves nothing. In fact, it can be damaging. As we shall see, the place to start is in the foothills among the people.

Interaction between the layers

The main characteristic of the power pyramid is how fluid the interaction is between the various layers. So MPs will hold a 'clinic' every week or so in their constituencies to hear the problems of the people. This 'keeping an ear to the ground' is essential. Certainly, the MP will get prior warning of local 'hot issues', but the clinic performs a number of other important functions:

- It is an opportunity for the MPs to show that they really are men or women 'of the people'. They come down to grassroots level and agree that the problems there are as important as the problems of state which they have to deal with in parliament.

- It stops issues getting out of hand; the MP can intervene at an early stage to stop a small problem becoming a major embarrassment.

- It is an excellent electioneering device; even for those MPs with safe majorities, there is always the fear that one day events may go against them or their party; for marginal MPs, the clinic is vital from the day they are elected.

- It allows them to meet the local councillors. Often constituents will first approach their councillor with a problem and then may accompany them to the MP's clinic. This is particularly so if the MP and the councillor are of the same party. This is highly impressive for the constituent and, even if the problem cannot be solved (in 99 per cent of cases), at least constituents feel they have been to the highest court there is. They have been taken seriously. This is a double win for the MP and for the councillor.

However, too often, organisations tend to think that the MP is the only person that matters. This is very dangerous. The foundations are more important than the roof.

As elections for parliament come around, this pyramid should turn into a well-oiled machine which the MP needs if he or she is going to get re-elected. In the case of new MPs, they may have come from the ranks of the councillors: in any event, this machine is needed to get elected.

In this campaign, the 'drill sergeants' or the canvassers are the county and district councillors. They will marshal people on the ground to write letters, raise funds and help persuade their friends to vote the right way on the day.

And when the council election comes around, a good MP will reciprocate the favour, working tirelessly to get his councillors into power in the local council.

Although looking simple from the outside the power pyramid is, in reality, more like a giant Heath Robinson machine. Our figure – messy as it looks – represents what could be considered an ideal case, but within it, there will be petty rivalries and jealousies, old scores to be settled, ambition, greed, altruism and hard work. In effect, a microcosm of human nature.

A slim majority

In national politics, we tend to talk of a slim majority for a parliamentary representative as being fewer than 5000 votes. At council level, few councillors who win a seat will poll a third of that amount. The following case shows how tightly balanced local politics can be at a number of levels. Power can hang on a knife edge and half-a-dozen votes.

DACORUM BOROUGH COUNCIL

Dacorum is a borough in Hertfordshire, a county to the north of London. The Council covers the major town of Hemel Hempstead, as well as the outlying towns of Berkhamsted, Tring and Kings Langley. For years the council had been controlled by the Conservatives, but the anti-Tory backlash of the late 1990s saw Labour gain a comfortable majority in 1995.

Just before the elections there was a split in the Labour ranks and four councillors defected to the Independents. (This is not uncommon in local politics.) However, with the help of the Liberal Democrats, Labour held onto power in the run-up to the election, although not having a clear majority.

The election campaign was a tough one and after nominations closed and campaigning began one of the candidates died. Under the rules, the election had to be suspended in that ward and the election would be held at a later date. The ward returned three councillors and was a solid Labour stronghold: they confidently expected to take all three seats.

This was the result of the election on May 7 1999.

Conservatives	26	
Labour	19	} 23
Liberal Democrats	4	
Vacancies	*3*	

DACORUM BOROUGH COUNCIL *(cont'd)*

So now the Conservatives had a majority of three. At the first council meeting, they elected the new mayor – naturally a Conservative. At the by-election, a few weeks later, Labour won all three seats, so now the Conservatives had 26 and the combined opposition had 26. However, the Conservative mayor still had the casting vote and so the Council was now under their control.

But if the unfortunate candidate had not died and Labour had won the three seats, what would have happened? The Conservatives would have had 26 and the combined Labour and Liberal Democrats would have had 26. A hung council again. But at the first meeting of the new council the out-going mayor would have had the casting vote and, as she was Labour, it would have remained a Labour council. (The Liberal Democrats would have supported Labour.)

But the knife edge is closer than that. Here are the results (in number of votes) of the five most closely contested seats in Dacorum:

Boxmoor

Marshall, JL	1015 (E)
Fairburn, AE	950 (E)
Hutchison, M	940

Nash Mill

Smedley, D	352 (E)
Fisher, SM	317

Berkhamsted Castle

Coleman, KJ	577 (E)
Ginger, PJ	542 (E)
Patterson, B	502
Corry, G	490

Tring Central

Rance, DM	639 (E)
Hollinghurst, N	581 (E)
Barnett, WG	530
Dawson, J	

Berkhamsted West

Sharpe, ST	604 (E)
Brooks, JHH	581 (E)
Reay, IM	572

There are a number of interesting factors here. First, the low turnout – it was only about 30 per cent. Second, the low number of votes per candidate. The highest for an elected candidate is 1015 and in Nash Mill 352 votes is enough to get elected. But even more remarkable is the size of the majorities of the elected candidates over their closest rivals: 9 votes, 10, votes, 25 votes, 40 votes and 51 votes. This is just a handful of people: In the first case, a largish family could have swung the vote. In all cases, a street voting a certain way would have made a huge difference.

From this, it is obvious that parish or community councils and residents' associations are powerful organisations – one street or issue can turn a poll. All councillors' majorities are always 'slim'.

Conclusion

Given the interplay in the power pyramid we saw earlier, delicate or difficult issues need to be treated with great caution. Not least by the politicians. They need to be fairly sure of their numbers. This is why politicians are often reluctant to make decisions or to come down on one side or the other. They cannot risk alienating significant minorities.

Careful decisions have to be made on delicate issues. And this is particularly so with issues relating to the environment. As we saw earlier, everyone has an environmental conscience or, at least, consciousness. This is a motherhood cause which politicians are very slow to run counter to. It is too dangerous.

7 The Stakeholder Diagnostic

Within a closed community the outsider quickly stands out. The stranger without local knowledge not only stands out, but he or she can be an affront to the very people they want to approach. The community's view may be: 'Not only don't you know us, you know nothing about us and yet you want to work with us and possibly damage our environment or lifestyle.' The first step in getting to know people is to have an understanding of their structure. The way to do this is through the diagnostic.

The need for local knowledge

When approaching people, especially politicians, it is important to have this local knowledge for a number of reasons:

- *Understanding*. The power pyramid is a complex organism. While from the outside it cannot be understood in all its complexity, at least a basic comprehension of the main elements – political and power-bases – is essential.

- *Respect and care*. Communities are all too familiar with organisations which arrive in their midst, take what they want or cause damage and then move on. In particular, cynical politicians are all too aware of the wiles of PR people and what they see as their smooth and oily ways. They also resent the single-project focus that organisations sometimes present. The impression is given that the only thing that really matters is 'the project'. Communities are complex, with many issues and local concerns. By being aware of these, it shows respect and care.

▪ *Dialogue and negotiation.* This understanding of a range of local issues is vital as one enters into what is essentially a negotiation. Most modern societies are also polite. It is unusual – even in business meetings – to jump straight into work-related matters. There is always a period of small talk where other issues – the weather, sport and the news of the day – are discussed. This allows the people in the meeting to settle in and get attuned and mentally prepared. In dealing with community representatives, this 'attunement' is all the more powerful if local issues can be discussed with understanding.

Put simply, taking the time and the effort to find out about local issues shows care, respect and a broader understanding of the community and its problems.

The diagnostic is a map

There are few people who would think of embarking on a long and complex journey without a map. There are whole shops devoted to maps and getting the right one is important. Here are the main problems with communications maps as they are used in attempts to identify stakeholders.

The wrong map
It would seem to be an obvious statement that one should ensure that one has the right map: for example, a map of Spain is of little use if one is visiting Italy. Yet that is exactly what happens in complex issues-related communication programmes. People rely on hearsay, stereotypes and gross misinformation when making decisions. When Christopher Columbus headed into the unknown in search of a route westwards to India, he and his crew were convinced that the seas were full of weird and wondrous monsters that could devour them. Similarly in complex communication programmes, rumours and hearsay build up about how antagonistic the natives are. People are very quickly labelled as friends (few) or enemies (numerous), often just because of one chance comment.

Old maps
Even worse, they rely on old and obsolete information. The restaurant and hotel guide produced by Michelin in 2000 will have very different listings from the one produced 50 years ago. Things change, people change. Look at political parties: who could have believed that socialist parties across Europe would not only allow privatisation of state industry, but actually

actively promote it, as is the case with Renault in France, not to mention the London Underground, Air Traffic Control and BNFL in the UK. And political maps change much more quickly than restaurant guides.

Maps of the wrong scale
Next, people take a map of the wrong scale. A general map of Europe is of little use if one is going hill-walking in the Alps. So, for example, it is assumed that just because a political party has a national policy on a certain issue, this is slavishly followed in the regions. Nothing is further from the truth. Political parties are broad churches: one has only to look at the UK Conservative Party members' totally differing views on the UK's role within Europe to understand this. In addition, some of the bitterness of national politics dissipates at local level. There are numerous dialogues across the political divide in local politics. Anecdotally, we know of many politicians who have better relations with some of the opposition than their own party colleagues.

This detailed map – called a diagnostic – is the first step in getting to know and understand the complex and difficult entity that is the power pyramid. However, for an organisation that wants to work with or within the pyramid, it is not only important to know and understand each of the layers, but more crucially to understand the interplay. Of course, as with all knowledge and understanding, this cannot happen instantly. It will take time: it is an organic process that will grow as one gets to know people on the ground. Before one can approach people, one needs a certain amount of knowledge.

To a greater or lesser degree, most modern democracies have a fairly open form of government where information is freely available. In addition, there is free press that for the most part is unfettered.

These two factors mean that there is a huge amount of information in what is generally called the public domain. Yet this information is for the most part ignored. Even worse, it is not collated into a useable form so that it can be applied.

From information available in the public domain, it is possible to put together a good map – on a number of scales, from the macro to the micro.

In politics the diagnostic is the first part of map-making. Ideally, this is done unobtrusively, without in any sense 'spying'. However, entering a community is not as easy as its sounds. There are a number of problems. Any stranger entering a tightly knit community will stand out like a sore thumb.

This background information is vital. Even if it does mean disturbing the placid millpond that characterises most communities, it must be garnered. And in as much detail as possible. On each project, we try to build a careful diagnostic of the community we are working in.

Without getting this information, we will always be the incomer, treated with caution and suspicion. Of course, merely having it is not enough in itself – in fact, far from it. But without it we cannot even make the first step.

Details of the diagnostic

Where (politically) is the site?
This may sound like a stupid question, but it is not. As we shall see, a site sits in a number of political contexts from its European or state representative right down to the parish council or commune. And all of these boundaries are not always the same.

We were briefed by a client on a site where they wanted to develop a new facility. He managed to get the parish wrong, the district council wrong and also placed it in the wrong county. As he wittily pointed out later: 'That's why I hired you guys.' So the first step must be to place the site accurately. In nine cases out of ten, this is simple, but with boundary sites it can be very difficult. Care is needed – simply because all the local people know exactly what is where and one's credibility is immediately damaged if simple facts like this are wrong.

Next, one needs to know who the key political and other players in the area are – they are the movers and shakers, the great and the good. This is all garnered from publicly available information. It should cover:

- the sitting member of the European parliament
- the sitting MP
- the previous MP if relevant, that is, if he or she is going to stand again
- the local county council; its political composition and track record
- the district or borough council; again politics and track record
- the local ward councillors for both the county and district; their view if known (through, for example, letters to newspapers, and so on)
- the local parish council or residents' association: its leading lights, views on issues, and so on
- local hot issues, the closure of a hospital or school, the need for new roads
- the local media – their campaigns and views
- local green groups – their campaigns and activities
- other relevant information.

THE VISIT TO THE LIBRARY

Local libraries are excellent places to begin this research. On a particular project, the library was in a tiny village and only open three days a week. By coincidence, one of our researchers was in the area on another piece of business meeting a senior figure in an adjoining council.

He decided to detour via the library. On arriving, he asked for some basic and publicly available materials: minutes of parish council meetings, press cuttings, back issues of the local newsletter and the like. These were provided and our researcher sat down to peruse the material, photocopying substantial amounts as he went along. The librarian busied herself with a number of tasks, including making several phone calls

Soon, the researcher noted that the library – very quiet on a mid-morning – was getting busier. A number of citizens of the village were casting furtive glances at him. Another was walking slowly past his car looking at it surreptitiously (but not acting suspiciously – she was in her early 70s). When he stood up to visit one of the shelves, another person materialised beside him and flicked aimlessly through a book. Over a period of two hours, half a dozen people cruised by him. Only much later, when the project was about to be launched, did he find out that he had just met most of the parish council, including the chairman and clerk.

Analysis
The moral is simple. Turning up in a small community dressed (as he was) in a smart business suit and making strange demands (no-one had asked for the parish council minutes in years) is bound to cause ripples in the pond. Our researcher may as well have come from Mars and parked a spaceship outside the library – he was that obtrusive.

Let us now work our way through some of these in turn, to see what a diagnostic might look like. It should be stressed that the following represents edited highlights and is not complete.

The local European parliament representative (probably equivalent to the senator in the USA)
Constituencies of the European parliament are huge – with hundreds of thousands of people in each one. Of course, if the project has a European dimension, then the relevance of the MEP will be proportionately greater. For most projects, the role of the MEP is not highly relevant. However, it is useful to know the agenda of this person: is he or she a keen environmentalist? what is his or her view of the trades union movement? and so on.

There is one key exception – if the project affects the area close to where the MEP lives. It is only human nature that we should take an interest in that which is most local – it would be folly to assume that MEPs – who have probably risen through local politics in any event – are any different.

The local parliamentary representative or member of parliament
(equivalent to congressman or woman in the USA)
The same comments apply as in the previous point, but the local parliamentary representative will take a much keener interest in events on the ground. They like to be aware of what is happening. If they have represented the constituency for any length of time, they will know it like the back of their hand. They will know all the movers and shakers in all parties.

The role of the sitting representative is important: he or she is the pinnacle of local political thought and these opinions matter. However, these opinions cannot run counter to those who elect them and it is important to remember that the foundation of these opinions lies with the regional district councils and community councils.

However, although there are those who believe that the democratic process can be influenced from the top, this is not so. Direct lobbying of the representative is usually a waste of time with a controversial project. Even if privately they could become advocates, they may not want to involve themselves in what they will see as highly localised issues.

However, one must be aware of where they live, what their opinions and their agendas are. The means of persuasion will be through those people on the local council they trust, respect and need – the drill sergeants mentioned in the power pyramid. The following is a detailed example of the section of a diagnostic showing how the representative can be placed in a local political context – the power pyramid – around the issues which concern them. (Obviously, this is a fictional case.)

THE SITTING PARLIAMENTARY
REPRESENTATIVE – GARRY GOODWIN (LABOUR)

Background
Garry Goodwin is the sitting MP for Old Town having won the seat from the Liberal Democrats in 1997. His majority is 3278 (6 per cent), which represented a substantial swing of 13 per cent. The seat is therefore very marginal.

The son of an architect, he is 55. He has spent many years trying to get elected to either Westminster or Europe. He contested the elections in Diamondshire in 1984,

THE SITTING PARLIAMENTARY REPRESENTATIVE *(cont'd)*

Mt Ommaney (Euro-MP) in 1986, Maidesville in 1989, Grassy Hill (MP) in 1992 and was finally elected to the Commons in 1997.

Garry Goodwin was born and educated in Surrey and gained a BEng from the University of Ripley. He then joined the University of Diamondshire where he rose through the ranks and was Head of the Engineering Department prior to his election.

Garry Goodwin is a member of the teachers' union, the NATFHE. He lists his interests as local government, green issues and the Third World.

For hobbies, he enjoys football, gardening, film and his family.

Parliamentary performance
Garry Goodwin is not one to latch himself onto controversial causes. He cannot afford to disaffect people. He seldom embroils himself in rows and is a great advocate of 'motherhood causes': schools, school transport, the local hospital, and so on.

In his maiden Commons speech, he (like most backbenchers) used a local issue – the need for maintaining the local school. (This school is under threat of being downgraded.)

Given that his seat is by no means safe, he spends much time on constituency affairs; so it is not surprising he does not have a particularly high profile in Parliament. Given the added factor of his age, he will not be on the list of high flyers. He only sits on one select committee, that of Trade and Industry.

He voted against the government on changes to the schools curriculum but otherwise he toes the party line.

Environmental interests
Garry Goodwin has recently agreed to speak for the Newts Society in the House of Commons. Given that Old Town's pond boasts the Great Crested Newt, this is worthy of very careful note.

He is a member of Greenpeace, although he does not seem to be active in any campaigns.

The next election
The party – at central level – will have made it clear that they see his re-election as his prime goal as, unlike some of the other marginals, this is winnable again at the next election. Therefore, he will be expected to have a strong constituency focus. His chances of retaining the seat are reasonable. Being the sitting MP gives Garry Goodwin an advantage – he can get things done. In addition, the opposition is in disarray.

At the next election, this seat will be fought bitterly. Both parties will have it on their list of key marginals, which means that it will be given extra resources.

THE SITTING PARLIAMENTARY REPRESENTATIVE *(cont'd)*

Analysis

There are a number of outcomes from this:

1. The role of the sitting parliamentary representative cannot be overstressed. He represents local thought and his opinions matter. However, these opinions cannot run counter to those who elect him – especially given his slim majority.

2. Garry Goodwin knows that he needs to run a well-orchestrated high-profile campaign if he is to win the next election. This means that he needs to motivate the troops on the ground. The marshalling sergeants are local councillors, so he needs to make sure his party is cohesive, undivided and motivated.

3. Having said that, however, he needs to draw in extra votes wherever he can get them. His membership of a green group is not accidental. He will be looking for stray green votes, as will all the rest. Within the cabinet, the green groups are given short shrift. They are seen as unelected, undemocratic power-hungry single-issue lobbyists. However, for individual representatives in tight marginals, this is overlooked.

4. The means of persuasion on this will be through those people on the local council he trusts, respects and needs. It is important to have defence strategies in place for him to use so that he can extricate himself when attacked.

The regional or county council

The next level of power is the regional council. Depending on which country one is in, this power varies enormously. Often this power is historical. For example, Italy only loosely united in the middle of the 20th century and still has a strong regional structure where the central government has reduced influence. Hence Italy – despite having a government a year since the Second World War – still manages to govern itself in its own fashion.

The USA has developed many power layers down to state level and further. States can set taxes and behave autonomously. Similarly the federal system in Germany – modelled after the Second World War on that in the USA – sees high levels of federal power. On the contrary, in the UK, the power of local councils was gradually whittled away in the 1980s by the then Prime Minister, Margaret Thatcher. Although councils have had much of their tax-gathering powers either removed or curtailed, they still have huge influence and, in a project where there is likely to be substantial community impact, they will almost have the right of veto – often through the planning system.

In many countries, there is a dual system of local government with a county council (department in France or canton in Switzerland) and the more local district councils.

The following is a diagnostic extract for a county council.

DIAMONDSHIRE COUNTY COUNCIL

Overview

Diamondshire is a hung council. The representation is:

Labour	18
Liberal Democrats	8
Conservatives	25

This is obviously very tight. Labour and the Liberals have formed an administrative coalition and now hold a one-seat majority on the council. Until 1993, this was a solid Conservative council when it first became hung, with the Liberals holding 13 seats. They had a reversal of fortune at the last election to leave the current situation. The next elections are not until 2001, but all it takes is one by-election to change the balance of power.

The council continues to remain very nervous about all environmental issues. The Conservatives are continuing to try to make life as difficult as possible for the Labour/Liberal Democrat coalition. Although, for the main part, their role in this current project is now played, this political bickering will continue with the Conservatives taking the moral high ground on this issue.

Analysis

The county council is not the on-the-ground decision-making body on this issue. It has laid down strategy at a broad level and this has now been agreed. Some major plans have now been agreed on environmental issues, so, in many ways, the county council has no further influence, except a huge power of nuisance, particularly if there is a change in the balance of power.

The local member for the county council

The local member is Barbara Jameson. She is the wife of Roger Jameson (the local district councillor for Melchester District Council) – see next extract. However, given that both the county council and the district council are Labour controlled and both she and her partner are (obviously) members of the Labour groups, this does not have much significance.

She sits on a number of powerful committees, including policy and planning, and is widely tipped to be group leader after the next elections when Jimmy McIntyre is expected to step down. If – and this is a BIG if – the Labour/Liberal Democrat coali-

DIAMONDSHIRE COUNTY COUNCIL *(cont'd)*

tion holds power, then she will be in a very strong position. How strong that influence will be on her partner remains to be seen.

Her majority of 347 votes leaves her in a reasonably secure position.

The district council

In regional government, one often finds that power is devolved to the district, borough or city level. In many cases, this is the decision-making body on controversial projects, so it is extremely important that it is carefully analysed.

MELCHESTER DISTRICT COUNCIL

The district council is responsible for housing (provision of council housing, homelessness), planning (planning applications for individual properties, change of use extensions, district or local plans, conservation and land use), leisure, parks and amenities and environmental health (including noise nuisance, markets, control of office, shop and factory premises).

The results of the recent elections for the district council leave the council with the following make-up:

	Last election	Previous
Labour	23	27
Conservatives	18	13
Liberal Democrats	2	2
Independents	1	2

Labour managed to maintain their strong hold on the council, winning 23 of the council's 44 seats – a result which surprised many of their followers. The party lost only four seats of those that they won in 1995 – one of which was Blackwell (nearby village).

The wards in and around the town are primarily Labour, with little changes bar a Conservative gain in Roystown (previously Independent) and an Independent gain in Blackwell (previously Labour).

MELCHESTER DISTRICT COUNCIL *(cont'd)*

Privately, local Labour politicians feared it was going to be much worse, expecting to lose anything between five and ten seats, and subsequently were delighted with the night's results.

While this may seem positive for Labour, it is also interesting to note that the electorate's enthusiasm for government and political processes has been somewhat apathetic, with only 35.2 per cent of eligible voters turning up to vote – a decrease of 10.7 per cent from the previous elections four years ago.

The local councillors
For the potential site, there are three wards affected. As with the regional council, a detailed analysis, as far as it is possible, is undertaken.

The parish, town council or commune
Again, these vary from country to country, but they are very powerful. In the UK, the parish or town council does not have a statutory role. However, they are always consulted on sensitive or controversial matters. These views of the real local people are listened to most carefully by the more senior politicians.

Often district councillors and, indeed, MPs, will also sit on these bodies so that they can keep their fingers on the pulse of local opinion. If there are going to be problems, it is here that they will start.

Not surprisingly, getting information in a non-intrusive way at this level is difficult. Some parish councils keep minutes only by writing them into a ledger maintained by the parish clerk. This is the only record! However, local libraries and the 'village notes' pages of the local paper can be very informative in this area.

Again, all of this needs to be analysed carefully. The following example shows the interplay between the various political players on a fictional site.

THE PARISH COUNCILS

Operations at the Stinkie landfill site affect three parish councils directly: Swinway, Whotford and Benwash. In addition, Benwash is the location for a controversial new

THE PARISH COUNCILS *(cont'd)*

bypass, which is strongly resisted locally. Some years ago, the merging of all three parish councils was considered but (probably because of internal wrangling) nothing came of it.

Swinway

The proposed extension to Stinkie landfill falls within this council's jurisdiction. This parish council covers a wide area with no real urban centre. The biggest population concentration is at the army camp. The council itself only meets six times a year. A presentation has been given to the council by the company (see file note).

The council is keen to stop 'rat running' between the roads around the site and has campaigned, although not actively, for this.

The clerk of the council – Mrs Joan Butcher – lives on Lovers Lane (one of the rat runs). The chairman is Mr Stuart Salmon, who is a local landowner and has dealt with the company in the past.

Whotford

This council probably gets most of the effects – particularly traffic – from the landfill operations. There is a perception that it continues on through the village, which it does not. By far the most vocal of the three parish councils, in particular when Mr Whyte was the chairman. There were a number of newspaper articles in which he was quoted on the traffic nuisance.

The new chairman of the council is Mr Frank Haxlett, a local businessman with interests in road haulage, although it should be stressed not in the village itself but in the nearby city. In particular, he will have an understanding of traffic issues – even if not a sympathy with the local situation.

The village feels under threat from the expansion of the local city and this is probably a bigger key issue than the landfill site.

Benwash

Little is known of Benwash at this stage and hopefully further investigations in the other two parishes – which are far more directly affected by the landfill operations – will give more information and an indication as to how they should be approached.

Other organisations

In addition, views should be taken on other local organisations, environmental groups and so on.

THE TOWN SOCIETY

The Town Society for Melchester is *very* active. They proudly claim to be the watchdog for the town, and indeed, they pop up far more often in the media than the parish council. The society is led by a committed and rigorous character, Commander Sir George Booth, who is also a county councillor. Many of the district councillors are also active in the society, including Roger Jameson and Jim Byrd.

The Town Society is mentioned regularly in the council minutes, in particular voicing objections to the planning committee on a plethora of applications. They act to inform locals of matters pertinent to the town, and usually include a message for action. They motivate and co-ordinate the town's millennium projects.

The hot issues

The diagnostic should also cover all the other hot issues in the locality, as well as any media campaigns that may be isolated.

TOWN CENTRE DECAY

On walking the high street of Melchester, there is an obvious absence of all the familiar elements. There are no high street clothing stores and in fact all of the shops are local businesses. The high street itself is very narrow and is constantly clogged with traffic trying to negotiate tight passes. There is also very little parking in the town. Both are issues which have been raised by the Town Society.

Local newspaper campaigns

Local newspapers try to gain an affinity with their readership for altruistic and purely financial reasons. This affinity holds old readers and attracts new ones. The following is a typical 'soft' campaign called 'Put Melchester on the Map'.

INTER-TOWN RIVALRY

Melchester feels it is the 'poor cousin' of other areas in the county. It is larger in population than Johnstown and yet no-one knows where it is. The newspapers are full of sentiments about the town being 'dumped' upon with all sorts of projects from waste disposal to new housing. On the opposite side of the coin, it believes it is being starved of investment at all levels from central government to regional authorities.

This is a soft campaign of which one should be aware. Harder campaigns involve the organisation of petitions against your project which, in the worst case, will also see the local MP roped into the anti-campaign.

Conclusion

The diagnostic is the map of the power pyramid. It is vital at the beginning to get an understanding of who the key stakeholders are or might be. Without it, one is travelling blind over a dangerous and sensitive landscape that is heavily landmined. However, like any good map, it is not an end in itself: it is but a beginning.

8 Launching and Managing Issues-related Projects

If you want to launch a new perfume, a new car and almost any other consumer product, the methodologies for doing it are fairly obvious. Because it is new, it is exciting. People will be curious, people will want it. Even cynical media will gush over it. However, for some reason, people cannot create the same sensation when launching a new incinerator, a piece of highly controversial legislation or plans to build a new prison or a hostel for people with AIDS. However, organisations still continue to use old, well-tried – and it has to be said, well-failed – methods of launching and managing controversial projects.

The DAD approach

The traditional way to announce projects can be summarised by the acronym DAD. This had three elements:

- **Decide** (always in private)
- **Announce** (without any consultation)
- **Defend** (refusing even the most minor changes).

The decide phase
For organisations this approach had many attractions. The decision phase could always be done in private. This allowed a neat technical solution to be devised without interference from amateurs or outsiders who had 'no real knowledge of the industry'. Often this means that purely technical solutions are adopted which do not take into account local sensitivities.

There are always many reasons why the technical solution – devised in-house – is not only correct but unalterable.

The announce phase

Large organisations generally have big marketing or communications departments and, if the company is to be successful, these departments have also to be successful. Therefore, it is not surprising that many of the techniques which are used in communications programmes are drawn from the world of marketing. However, as we will see in Part IV on communication tools, these will be of limited use in controversial projects where there is widespread opposition.

However, organisations are slow to change and still the same old mechanisms are used: the sudden announcement by press release, by dropping leaflets, by writing large numbers of letters to people one does not know or by large-scale advertising. This is an adversarial approach and, of course, there is often little or no pre-consultation on the ground.

The reason given for this (almost always) is that one does not want to lose the element of surprise. But do you like being surprised? Not everyone likes surprises, particularly when they are unpleasant. This so-called advantage of surprise quickly backfires and there is no surprise when there is immediate backlash, usually by people whose main complaint is lack of prior consultation.

These mass communications mechanisms are also very safe – they can be used from some distance and do not involve head-to-head clashes with people who might be affected. It is simple to drop a press release in the post to the local newspaper or to hold a press conference at company headquarters.

The defend phase

There then comes the defend phase and organisations are particularly adept at this – not only adept, but also one could say comfortable. Inevitably, the defend phase involves some form of public forum, where the organisation (as outlined in Part IV, when we also look at public consultation) is put in the stocks to have rotten apples thrown at it.

But this is a very safe and secure, if not a particularly pleasant, position. For a start, one controls the main means of communication: the podium from which one speaks as well as a slide or overhead projector which gives one some control of the agenda. Second, it is possible to train people to stand up and be shouted at. It's not enjoyable, but there is seldom a shortage of masochistic volunteers. Third, it does not involve one-to-one conflict, which most people abhor. It is one person against the mob – an

THE NUCLEAR DUMP SITES

If you use electricity in a country that generates nuclear power, then you are responsible for producing nuclear waste. Under the polluter pays principle, you have a duty to clear this mess up. In fact, almost everyone agrees with this. But the classic NIMBY response is always brought forward: we need to get rid of this stuff, but not near me.

In the mid-1980s, the UK's nuclear industry decided that it needed to find a location to build an underground repository for this radioactive waste. It hit on four sites (to this day the fiasco is known as the 'four site saga') all chosen for technical reasons, primarily because they had geology which was suitable to contain the waste for hundreds of thousands of years. Without any warning at all, these were announced to an unsuspecting public. This was done, quite properly, in the House of Commons and the first people in the four regions knew about it was while listening to the evening news. By midnight the action and protest groups had been formed.

The industry fought long and hard, but eventually the government – in the run-up to an election – lost heart and the sites were withdrawn.

Analysis
This was DAD in action. It was doomed to failure mainly because:

- the industry had no knowledge of the communities and the politics of the areas into which it was launching itself
- it had taken no time to find out what the needs and fears of these communities were
- the announcement was followed by a vacuum – there was no-one on the ground immediately to defend it.

It took days for the industry to get around to making approaches to local politicians. By that time, the agenda had been lost; fixed and unhookable positions had been taken. In fairness, it should also be said that with such a difficult subject, even the best campaign in the world would have faced terrible difficulties, particularly as the four sites chosen had almost no knowledge of the nuclear industry.

honourable position. Finally, when it is done, it is done. In most cases, it does not need to be repeated. The organisation can pat itself on the back and say: 'Well, that was tough but at least we have conducted a full public consultation exercise.'

Obviously, there must be another approach. In the last two chapters a segmentation of stakeholders was undertaken. In addition, the mechanisms surrounding a diagnostic were explained. From these exercises one can look to new ways of launching and managing issues-related projects.

Stakeholder segmentation – practical guidelines

Looking back at the stakeholder analysis completed in Chapter 5, we noted that there are five types:

1. *Dependent stakeholders*: employees, suppliers, and so on
2. *Impacted stakeholders*: for example those living near a facility
3. *Unknown stakeholders*: for example those who have not made themselves known
4. *Supporting stakeholders*: subsets of the last three categories
5. *Intractables*: those intractably opposed.

However, stakeholder mapping or analysis is useless if it is an academic exercise, which is undertaken as a stand-alone research project. Too often, it is used to find out who an organisation's enemies are. This is the worst possible use of such mapping. Of course, it does isolate the intractable stakeholders, but they are only a tiny minority, usually unrepresentative and with their own agendas. If mapping is undertaken to isolate these so that they can be 'dealt with' (in either sense of that phrase), the beginning of the end is near. As we saw, to try to achieve consensus with one's enemies is a waste of time – they just want to get close enough to you to kill you.

No, a key objective of the stakeholder analysis is to find those who may be able to help the organisation. This research must be applied to be of benefit – it must be put into action.

In particular, it must be used to isolate the special group we call the supporter stakeholders or third party advocates (TPAs), drawn from each of the dependants, the impacted or the unknowns.

Every organisation can divide its stakeholders into these groupings. In our experience, this can be a fairly simple and, indeed, enjoyable exercise.

Step 1. Undertake the diagnostic
The level of detail needed has been outlined in the last chapter. However, the diagnostic is not revealed at this stage. If it was, it would tend to skew the exercise and would hinder the coming forward of the unknown stakeholders in particular, who are often critical.

Step 2. Form a brainstorming group
The next step is to bring together a group of six to ten people with an independent moderator, who has a working knowledge of the company and who can guide and direct the group in its deliberations. It is important

that the moderator is external as otherwise old turf wars may be fought in the session. Care is needed in bringing this group together. It should be wide ranging and include a number of disciplines. For example, the group should not consist only of members of the PR department. Ideally, it could include:

- Someone with first-hand front-line operational experience, especially if they had been involved in a contentious issue and have some scars

- Human resources departments can bring an internal/employee dimension

- Research and development people (if they exist) can bring a more existential feel which in its blind rationality can often bring the group back to earth: the 'facts are facts so what is the problem?' approach

- Outside consultants (no more than one of these – otherwise they start competing), particularly from the lobbying field

- Someone fairly senior from the public relations department – if the project is being 'led' by PR, then it should be this person.

The group should definitely not be more than ten (six is not a bad number), otherwise it turns into a mob and can run out of control. The objective is to get as wide a range of views as possible. (Eventually, this may form the basis of a project steering group, which will be dealt with later in the chapter. However, this initial brainstorming group can – and should – involve people who are well outside the project and may have no other involvement in it after this exercise. This is to ensure as wide a range of inputs as possible.)

Step 3. Stakeholder search
The moderator asks the group members to name who they believe to be stakeholders in the company. Each of these names is written on a large piece of card. Post-it notes are too small – it is important that the card can be read from a distance. At this stage, no names are ruled out. The objective is to get as wide ranging a list as possible. Individuals as well as organisations are welcome and the moderator makes this clear. At the end of this part of the exercise, there should be a substantial number (sometimes many hundreds) of names.

When this phase has been exhausted, the moderator brings forward the key names which have been isolated by the diagnostic. What is really amazing is that most of these names mean nothing to the group. They are just names on a list.

Step 4. Stakeholder positioning
Then the group is asked to say whether the stakeholders as outlined are friends, enemies, neutral or 'don't know'. This is always a fascinating part of the exercise. A good moderator will challenge each assumption and ask for concrete reasons for each categorisation. Only when there is specific evidence and the entire group accepts the categorisation is an organisation or individual labelled. What is intriguing from this is the lack of knowledge of the stakeholders. You will hear phrases such as: 'I was always under the impression that...' or 'I remember they had a particularly vocal member who gave us a lot of trouble some years ago...'. Individuals cannot, unless they are nominated to do so, represent an organisation. So for example, if a local councillor who was a member of the Liberal Democrat group spoke out against a new road, it would be very wrong to assume that all his party was now anti-roads. He may have been speaking in an individual capacity, because it went past his aunt's front door.

Step 5. Stakeholder categorisation
The cards are then regrouped into one of the five categories:

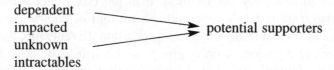

As noted earlier, it is amazing how big the unknown category turns out to be. It is important that this exercise is done openly and that everyone agrees – hence the large cards mentioned earlier.

At this stage, the work is not finished. There are more potential stakeholders who need to be isolated. This forces the group to think laterally and positively along the lines of:

■ Who else might be able to help you?
■ What other organisations are in the same position as yourself?
■ Who are the key individuals?
■ Have they always been that way?
■ What would be needed to change their minds?
■ And many, many more questions.

In this last part of the exercise the real surprises begin to emerge. Organisations which were not even considered as being relevant suddenly seem like potential friends, as the following example shows.

THE WARRING QUARRIES

Quarrying for minerals and aggregates is always a contentious business. Unless the quarrying company does its community relations well, local people and their representatives can work against the interests of the operator. Licensing authorities too take a keen interest, particularly in how the quarry will look after the company has finished. Large holes gouged out of the ground are no longer acceptable. The company's plans for restoration are as important as its plans for operating the quarry in the first place.

The business is on the verge of being a commodity, so margins are tight; and rivalries between companies are strong and deep.

Quarrymasters Ltd had applied to the local licensing authority to extend its quarry for another five years. However, this was not in accord with the five-year plan whereby the licensing authority saw no further development. Quarrymasters' existing quarry adjoined another operating quarry run by Top Aggregates. The company was at an impasse.

After a segmentation exercise, Quarrymasters' staff put Top Aggregates firmly in the intractables box: 'They want us out of business' was the opinion. After a number of meetings with local politicians and the licensing authority, it became obvious that the latter's main concern was not the extension to the quarry, but a joint restoration plan for both quarries so that they would integrate together when both companies were finished.

Now, licensing authorities are powerful and Quarrymasters agreed that it would consider a joint restoration proposal with Top Aggregates. This would improve relations with the licensing authority for both companies and would facilitate the extension for Quarrymasters.

Analysis

After meetings between the two companies a joint way forward was quickly found. This involved not only a joint restoration plan but also an agreement to work jointly the new extension to the quarry. So, from a point where Top Aggregates was an intractable opponent, it had moved to being a key dependent stakeholder. It turned out that the company's arch-rival, which it had hardly spoken to in years, was now a key supporter of its project.

The basic message is not to categorise from past behaviours and always be prepared for surprises. Supporters can be found in the most unlikely places, but they need to be cultivated and this takes time.

LITTLE BOXES, LITTLE BOXES

In the Western world, as the levels of prosperity continue to rise, so do our expectations from our environment (Chapter 2). A classic case of this is the house-building industry.

Prior to the Second World War (1939–45), the standard of housing, particularly for what was then called the working classes, was very poor. Internal sanitation was far from universal and quality of the housing stock was poor. The war damaged much of this housing, in particular in inner city areas, and the call went out to rebuild Britain and to provide 'houses fit for heroes'. There was a caveat: that a number of cities should have a 'green belt' around them – especially London. This was a crude but effective device to stop urban sprawl.

Much of the new building was undertaken by local authorities where functionality was the prime driver rather than design. The private sector took a similarly robust view and houses were built as houses. In both cases, little thought was given to design – either in terms of house type or the environment in which the house would be located.By the end of the century, it was a different world. Design and quality had improved beyond recognition and the increasing powers of development control or planning departments had ensured carefully designed developments. But amazingly, where once people had welcomed houses, something far more radical had changed. House-building was no longer popular. Especially if it was near me: the not in my back yard (NIMBY) syndrome.

NIMBYism of the 1980s, based on pure self-interest, had changed tack by the mid-1990s. Now it was all about protecting the environment. 'It's not that we don't want new houses,' the argument would run, 'it is just that this is such a beautiful part of the country. It would be a shame to spoil it. Build the houses somewhere less sensitive.'

This shift to environmental protection is a clever move and neatly catches the mood of the age. Even *The Times* of London has run a 'Greenfield campaign', seeing that it locks into a favourite concern of its readership. In particular, the fight is on to protect the green belt.

So, for a developer who wants to build houses in the green belt, how might a stakeholder audit look?

Table 8.1	Political mapping for a house-building company
For	*Against*
The developer	*Political*
The developer's employees	The local member of parliament
The House Builders' Federation	The local council
Suppliers of building materials	The parish council
Local suppliers of these materials	The residents' association
Building workers	
The government – which sees the need for many new houses into the future	*Environmental groups*
	Council for the Protection of Rural England – nationally
	Council for the Protection of Rural England – local chapter
	Friends of the Earth
	Greenpeace
	EarthFirst!
	URGENT! – an umbrella anti-housing group
	Interest groups
	The civic society
	The local residents
	The yet-to-be-formed action group – no doubt with an acronym as a title, such as Save Our Fields Today (SOFT)

First, let's take a rough cut of those who are for and those who are against. This is the classical way of 'political mapping' (Table 8.1).

On the face of it, the best thing the developer could do is go away. There certainly are powerful forces ranged against the project.

But now let's look at these stakeholders using a different analysis and let us see what we know of them in terms of the levels of their support or opposition using the new stakeholder analysis (Figure 8.2): we now have a very different picture. Certainly, the opposition has not changed, neither have the supporters, and if we look at them in numerical terms, they are about equal. Certainly, the opponents are better organised, but whose fault is that? They are also more vocal, but one expects that. As we saw earlier their main role in life is public relations, so we expect them to be good at it.

Even if there are other groups out there who oppose, they will very quickly make themselves known. It is not a characteristic of those who oppose to remain silent. So what do we do with them? We politely ignore them. In the words of a former American President, Lyndon Baines

Table 8.2 An analysis of the stakeholders using the new analysis				
Dependent	*Impacted*	*Unknown*	*Intractables*	*Supporters*
The developer	Suppliers of building materials	Building workers		Yes
The developer's employees	Local suppliers of these materials			Yes – as far as they are aware
The House Builders' Federation				Yes
The government				Yes
	The local member of parliament			Don't know – he or she may be against housing in general but maybe not against a specific scheme
	The local council			Don't know – Generally anti-building in green belt, but some schemes have gone through
	The parish council			Don't know – same as the council
	The residents' association			Don't know
		The civic society		Don't know
	The local residents			Don't know – they have not been asked
	The yet to be formed action group(SOFT)			Don't know – they have not been asked
		Organisations we do not know about		Can't know – Don't know
		People/individuals we do not know about		Can't know – Don't know
		Things and events we do not know about		Can't know – Don't know

			Table 8.2 (cont'd)	
Dependent	*Impacted*	*Unknown*	*Intractables*	*Supporters*
			Council for the Protection of Rural England – nationally	Against
			Council for the Protection of Rural England – local chapter	Against
			Friends of the Earth	Against
			Greenpeace	Against
			EarthFirst!	Against
			Urgent! – an umbrella anti-housing group	Against

Johnson, who had particularly apposite advice for an opponent to his plans: 'Why don't they take a flying ∗∗∗∗ at a rolling doughnut?' Indeed. As we saw earlier these opponents only want projects to fail. Every tiny concession they gain is a victory for them and a loss for you. Have as little as possible to do with them. They will drain your resources.

Certainly, one should be polite and respond to all reasonable requests, for instance, for information. However, requests to attend a public meeting they organised should be refused. Requests to attend a public meeting organised by the local council, with a leader councillor as the chairman, should be agreed to. After all, these are not avowed opponents. (For how to handle these events, see Part IV.)

What is most interesting is all these 'don't knows'. But, it may be asserted that these people's views are already known – they have been vocal in the past. But remember that each project is different, people are allowed to change their minds on specific projects. There is always an exception that proves the rule.

In classical public relations, these don't knows are assumed to be opponents based on their past record and their public pronouncements. This is a fatal assumption and the main reason why most difficult projects go off track. The moment you assume someone is an enemy, he or she automatically becomes one. There is no way back from this road – battle lines are quickly drawn and now it is war. War wounds are slow to heal. Often these dangerous assumptions put people who might support a project into the enemy camp.

Many of these individuals and organisations can help, but they are often either ignored or bypassed. There is only one way to find out what they really think – ask them. The methodology for doing this is outlined later in this chapter. When one begins to listen, it is amazing what can be discovered, as this case illustrates.

THE NEW COMMUNITY CENTRE

A major company owned substantial amounts of land in the green belt. This was historical but of little use to the firm, as they could not do much with it. It was highly unlikely that it would ever be anything but fields with minimal agricultural value.

This was an articulate middle-class area with strong opposition to further development of housing in the vicinity of the local village. For the land owner, this was near a lost cause. The company had operated previously in the area and as part of an audit of these operations (for a community relations programme) we were asked to review the company.

We began to speak to people in an informal way, and soon it became apparent that the village had no proper community facilities. The problem was not money, it was land. The village could not afford to buy land at commercial rates – almost 25,000 times the agricultural rate.

After some time, it became apparent to the village's community leaders, including the parish council and the local councillor, that there was the possibility of a win–win deal. This would mean that land would be given for the community centre. However, the land owner would also be allowed to develop a small amount of land for housing.

The parish council and local residents and politicians immediately began to support this project. Naturally, they maintained their total opposition to 'wide-scale' development of the village into the green belt.

And because the local people were in favour, the green groups chose not to get involved. They are clever: there is little merit in fighting popular causes. Certainly, they tried to lobby behind the scenes, but in this case the strength of feeling on the ground neutralised their efforts.

Analysis
This case history did not involve one public meeting, one press release or one bit of lobbying. However, this is a classic case of the use of third party advocates. There were those within the village who wanted something. People are very reasonable, almost everyone accepts that anything worthwhile in life cannot be free. There must be a price. If they believe that the price is worth paying then they will pay it – willingly. In fact, they will become advocates.

THE NEW COMMUNITY CENTRE *(cont'd)*

How about the land owner? Certainly, he wants to gain from this deal and negotiated hard to get what he wanted.

Contrast this case to the DAD strategy, which is the classical methodology. In this case, the land owner would have announced that he is to build a new community centre. As part of this announcement, he would 'bury' the fact that there would be a 'small' housing development attached. Now what is small? In astronomical terms, it is a planet the size of the earth. Unquantified adjectives are the most dangerous tool in a press release – next to the press release itself.

The would-be DAD developer has to show all the cards on Day 1. Now there is no room for flexibility without loss of face and a complete backsliding on the project. Because a project actually exists, people are immediately forced to take sides. The day after the announcement, the decision has to be made – are you for or against it? As C Northcote Parkinson put it so eloquently: 'The vacuum produced by a lack of information is quickly filled by rumour, innuendo, lies and drivel.' But, protests the developer, we put out a press release and wrote to the local council and councillors. Waste of time – that is not information, that is propaganda and no-one believes propaganda.

Now comes the next problem: bribery. There is only one thing worse than giving a bribe and that is accepting one. So what is the developer trying to do with the new community centre? It is trying to bribe the people and the people will resent it. If the project does not go well – and it probably won't – the developer will say: 'Well, if we cannot build our houses, then you will never get your community centre.' Replacing one 'B' word with another – bribery with blackmail – is a sure route to failure.

Of course, people want to have inputs into projects that shape their lives. And they have elected representatives who *represent* their views. And if they have inputs, then they have ownership. And if they have ownership, it becomes *their project* and so they will fight for it.

These independent people on the ground are the cornerstone for success in any controversial project and yet they are so often ignored.

The approach outlined here is a truly democratic approach. The people decide what they want and the terms under which they are willing to accept it.

As opposed to DAD, this approach is called CHARM, which is rather appropriate in an industry that specialises in acronyms. It stands for Consult, Harmonise, Adjust, Reinforce and Maintain.

Let us look at each of these five elements in turn.

Consult

Before one even thinks about launching a project, one must consult on the ground. Certainly, there is the risk that the details of the project may leak. But what is this fascination about stopping things leaking? Everything leaks and there is a simple rule: the more sensitive it is, the more likely it is to leak.

Why are organisations fixated that the details of some big project will leak when they plan to announce it at a huge press conference the next day? Surely the leak is helping with their work? Certainly, it messes up the nice plans for the chief executive to make his or her grand announcement and this may affect the career opportunities of the PR director. But if something is going to happen anyway, there is no need for secrecy. As we saw in the previous chapter, by consulting on the ground, all sorts of information comes to light. Indeed, all sorts of helpful people are found.

Harmonise

The project as originally formulated is often not acceptable. It is not that there is necessarily anything wrong with it: it is just that people on the ground have no ownership of it; it is not harmonised with their expectations. Their views have to be taken on board. As we saw this is very difficult for companies.

Adjust

This can be the most difficult bit: how do you persuade the chief engineer that her beautiful creation, on which she has worked for seven years, will have to be adjusted. The word 'adjust' is important here. It is not change. This is an *adjustment* to an already existing project; change is when we start all over again with a brand new project. Those who suggest change are opponents of the scheme; those who suggest adjustments are supporters. (The harmonisation and adjusting phases are covered in Chapters 9 and 10.)

Reinforce

The project has been launched and the supporters and third party advocates are in place on the ground to defend it. But they are under immediate attack. They did not expect the opponents to be so vociferous. They are accused of selling out. They will be under threat; they will accused of feathering their own nest; of self-aggrandisement. Here they will need support and reinforcement. Without this they will begin to wither.

The organisations must have mechanisms in place to take the heat off. This may mean taking some of the brunt of the attacks upon itself. There are crucial times when the third party advocates on the ground need professional supporters and techniques. They may need help to draft letters, to write press releases, whatever. The organisation must be ready to jump in to do these things.

Maintain
Very difficult projects take time and if they are not maintained, the third party advocates will lose interest, they will move on to other things. Also, controversial projects can run over a number of years. It is vital to maintain the momentum; to continue to provide the support and reinforcement. Too many projects are launched and then the company moves away, leaving the field open to the opponents who quickly take it over. Launching controversial projects is a difficult business and maintaining the momentum, often in the face of vast opposition, is a Herculean task.

Practical guidelines

The CHARM approach is systematic and methodological. There are a number of steps:

1. Undertake a diagnostic (Chapter 7)
2. Undertake the stakeholder segmentation exercise as outlined earlier
3. Isolate the key people who are involved and approach them
4. Understand the communication tools that may be used and their limitations (Part IV)
5. Find the win–win projects and third party advocates to act for them (Chapter 9)
6. Get third party advocates to champion the project (Chapter 10).

The last part of this exercise is the most difficult. Why? Because we are all enthused by new projects, but we quickly lose interest. TPAs get side-tracked by other projects. They face huge pressure from the opposition. But one of the main reasons is that the organisation itself tends to lose interest.

People move on, are promoted or move to other organisations; another project becomes flavour of the month. In long-running projects boredom sets in.

The project steering group

Therefore, it is important to have a systematic way to keep the project on course. This can have many names but, for this exercise, let's simply call it the project steering group (PSG). While one is always reluctant to suggest forming a 'committee' as the first step, if this is not done the project will fail for a number of reasons:

- it will be seen as an individual's initiative
- it will ignore key players
- it will be undermined by opponents.

In addition, there are sound practical reasons for the steering group:

- it sets objectives and targets for the work to be undertaken
- it monitors progress
- it provides a forum for the sharing of ideas.

The project steering group should meet once a month. While it should not meet any less frequently, it can certainly meet more often as the need demands. It should be a small group – five or six is ideal. It should have an outside facilitator who looks after the agenda, minutes, reports, and so on. Outside facilitators are important for a number of reasons:

- they bring independence
- they can intervene in internal faction fighting and office politics. In fact, the mere presence of an outsider stops this
- they let the group get on with other work when the project is quiet and the facilitator can maintain focus.

Members of the project steering group

The group must be multi-disciplinary, otherwise it will not function well. (It may include some of the members of the brainstorming group mentioned at the beginning of this chapter.) The chairman may not necessarily be the project director, but it should be someone who is fully committed to the project and has the time to devote to the group. There is nothing worse than a chairman who attends only every second meeting and has to be constantly brought up to speed at each alternate meeting.

A typical group could look like this:

Director of communications (chair)
Senior technical manager
Senior PR or HR manager (to handle internal communications as
  necessary)
Community liaison manager/press officer
External facilitator.

The first meeting

While projects vary, the first meeting should have on its agenda some, if
not all, of the following:

1. A technical summary of the project.

2. Why it may be difficult in environmental, community or other terms.

3. An early view of who the key players on the ground might be:
   - the potential supporters
   - the opposition
   - the don't knows.

4. A first cut of the politics:
   - the diagnostic should be commissioned at this stage for report back
     at the next meeting.

The second meeting

Again, stressing that this is idealistic, a second meeting could have as its
agenda:

1. The diagnostic – report back:
   - who are the key politicians – at national and local levels
   - what is the party politics
   - who are the other key movers and shakers in the area
   - what is the view of the media of other events; is there a strong green
     or anti-development stance, for example?
   - other information.

2. The results of the brainstorming exercise:
   - who are seen as key potential supporters at this stage?

3. What is the forward strategy?:
   - what is needed in political and community terms to make sure this
     project moves ahead in a timely way?

- what is needed to get third party advocates on the ground?
- what people and organisations must be met to be sounded out on project?

The steering group should consider this list and begin to prioritise and personalise it. They will also have other organisations and names to add – the list is very much a starting point. What does the group know about this organisation and, more importantly, who does it not know? What does it think its priorities are? How can they be motivated to act? What could they do? What might they want in return? From this exercise, a list will evolve on which actions can be taken. This meeting will take some time (about half a day) as there are always fairly intensive debates.

4. What are our limits of negotiation? This should be led by the technical director. What concessions can be made? The point is not to give them at this stage, but at least to have some understanding of the limits of flexibility. If there is none, then some should be built in. In other words, ask for more than is needed, so that it can be negotiated away later.

The third meeting

At this stage, some three or four local people have been met. From here, a much deeper understanding of the local community and its win–win project is beginning to come to the fore. This is covered in the next chapter.

Conclusion

Empowering people – especially key stakeholders – is a highly democratic way of managing projects. It will also bring results, By giving people control of their own environment, they can provide real win–win projects that work for them and the promoting organisation.

9 Finding Third Party Advocates

It is well accepted that satisfied customers – making recommendations for a company's products – are very powerful. In the last chapter, we saw that it will be these third party advocates (TPAs) who will be an essential part of driving the project. But first they must be identified.

The power of TPAs

For years, the giant retail chain Marks & Spencer refused to use one of the main planks of marketing – advertising. Instead, it relied on its reputation for quality, fair play to customers (for example, exchanging goods without quibbling) and the recommendations of its many satisfied customers. Certainly, that company has hit tough times, but these are less to do with marketing and more to do with other aspects of management.

The green groups are also very good at finding their own third party advocates. The frozen goods supermarket chain, Iceland, was very happy to attack Monsanto on behalf of the green movement, so associating itself with it for its own gain.

The cosmetics chain, the Body Shop, is closely allied with the green groups and became deeply involved in the attack on Shell over its policies in Nigeria. In fact, the Body Shop won a PR award for this and – by association – Greenpeace nearly won one too, much to its embarrassment. After all, Greenpeace always protests loudly that it is not in the PR business. In fact, of Greenpeace's total budget of £100 million, almost all is devoted to PR – even though it may be called campaigning, it's the same thing. The Shell campaign on Brent Spar cost some £2 million and used some of the most sophisticated transmission equipment in the world. Not in the PR business, indeed!

In fact, many PR consultancies and professionals could easily take a leaf from the green groups' books and not even enter PR awards, much less try to win them. After all, PR is widely seen as something that is done to improve perceptions – put cruelly, it is rather like papering over a cracked wall. Organisations need to present themselves as being solidly constructed, not experts at interior decoration. Ironically, to be seen to be good at PR damages your case.

These word of mouth recommendations – or references by third party advocates – are powerful for a number of reasons.

Trust
Recommendations generally come from friends or colleagues who are trusted. The person who is making the recommendation is known. For example, if one is contemplating buying a car, a colleague who is known to have an interest in this area may be approached. Certainly, one may also buy car magazines, take greater note of advertising and read press articles, but this individualised recommendation is very powerful. There is this huge level of trust which cannot exist in an outside source.

Independence
The person making the recommendation is independent – they have no real financial interest. Almost all other forms of communication do not have this. Taking the motor car example again, advertising is obviously paid for by the manufacturer, and it is well known that almost all motoring journalists receive free cars from the manufacturers to 'test'. In fact, some journalists have cars on semi-permanent loan in order to perform long-term tests. Therefore, it is hardly surprising that many of the columns which emerge from this process are not particularly scathing of the products – suggestions that the ashtray might be moved half a centimetre is often the harshest criticism.

Local knowledge
The person making the recommendation knows the person he has given the advice to. With the car, he knows the family circumstances (number of children, dogs, and so on), the aspirations of the would-be owner (image versus safety, for example) and so can advise on that basis.

However, the task of finding these third party advocates looks almost impossible if one is managing a large project or, worse, a number of projects. In addition, for most organisations with controversial issues to manage, they are either remote from the physical location or else they have a number of locations to deal with. It certainly is difficult to get on the ground and be local when one has to deal with 150 sites. Most organisations are daunted by this task and rely instead on the traditional communications methods – press releases, leaflets, public meetings and exhibitions. There is also a misconception that these methods are cheap. A leaflet, which is distributed to thousands of homes, costs only fractions of a penny. But then the difficult questions must be asked:

- How many people picked it up?
- How many people glanced at it?
- How many people read it carefully?
- How many people believed it?
- How many people decided to take a positive action for the project?

The answer to these most important last two questions is almost always zero. So then why bother? Press releases suffer a similar fate. (Certainly, these communication tools have their uses – and limitations – and are dealt with in Part IV.)

However, these mass media approaches totally ignore the democratic system, which greatly simplifies matters. Within every community there are elected *representatives* – and that word must be stressed – who have been chosen to represent the views of the people. In addition, there are others who have power by dint of their position: industry leaders (chambers of commerce), religious leaders, and so on. In fact, sending leaflets to members of the public could be seen as an attempt to bypass the democratic system (see Part IV).

This excellent system immediately brings a project into terms which are manageable, yet it is so often totally ignored.

Why TPAs remain hidden

Having isolated potential supporting stakeholders, they are absolutely useless if they sit on the fence and do nothing. The scientists who worked on genetically modified crops in universities and did not speak out are a typical example. Why? Because no-one asked them, or if they did, they were not given the necessary incentives (and we are not talking about money here) to do so.

So why do people – often real experts – not speak out? There are a number of reasons:

- *Modesty.* Although the mantra in the academic world is 'publish or perish', academics are often reluctant to put their head above the parapet. (There are some obvious well-known exceptions who, to protect their modesty, we will not mention here.) However, we all have a reluctance to be 'pushy'. These modest people will certainly berate the poor and inaccurate coverage in the media, but they would not think of writing a letter to a newspaper to correct that inaccurate report.

- *Institutional restraint.* It is not only in large companies that employees are discouraged from airing their views to a larger audience; the same applies in many academic and research organisations. Often there is a complex committee structure to be negotiated, before an 'agreed statement' can be issued. This can take many weeks and be so surrounded in caveats to be both content-free and useless. In the words of Ronald Reagan: 'Give me one-handed economists', to avoid the phrase 'On the other hand…'.

- *Fear of isolation.* 'Breaking from the pack' is unnatural. There is a fear of being left in the open, particularly if it is a contentious or unpopular cause.

- *Ridicule.* Those who take on the green groups, who present themselves as latter-day saints with no faults, do so at some risk to their own personal credibility. To take on the guys in the white hats is not easy.

- *Peer pressure.* We are slow to take and espouse a view which might not necessarily meet with the approval of our peers.

- *Lack of incentive.* It is human nature to think: 'What's in it for me?' Theoretically, we are not supposed to take such a non-altruistic view, but it is so. Just ask the people in Greenpeace, whose wages are equal, or above industry average.

Many of these individuals and organisations can help, but they are often either ignored or bypassed. There is only one way to find out what they really think – ask them, and the methodology for doing this is outlined in the next chapter. When one begins to listen, it is amazing what can be discovered.

Who might be a TPA?

From Chapter 7, we have two powerful tools: the stakeholder audit and the diagnostic. The diagnostic is an essential map of the project. To start without it is like setting off on a round-the-world trip without an atlas. Yet, it is amazing how many projects, which need political goodwill to succeed, fail to take this elementary precaution from the beginning.

The stakeholder audit has given us a view of who might be important within the scope of the project. More importantly, it has begun to isolate those people who might be willing to support the project – almost certainly with conditions.

From these pieces of work, there is now a two-dimensional view of the site. Like making a jigsaw puzzle, one starts with the edges and then trics to fill in the inside detail. As everyone who has done a jigsaw knows, thc edges are the easiest.

However, the stakeholder audit and the diagnostic serve only to give an overview – rather like a general map of a country, it does not show the small towns and villages, the local roads and pathways. Certainly, it looks detailed, but it is missing an essential dimension – what people really think – especially those important people who may support the project. It is rather like a scientific theory that has not been proven by practical work in the laboratory.

In effect, the work in the stakeholder audit and the diagnostic is two-dimensional. In order to make it three-dimensional, it is important to verify and clarify the conclusions reached. The way to do this is to talk to people on the ground, those people who have been identified from the diagnostic. Again, these views are always surprising and new information always comes to light to alter one's thinking yet again.

In particular, one gets a view of where the real levers of power lie. What is always interesting about this exercise is that it gives results that were unexpected. Sometimes the TPAs do not directly hold the levers of power, but they are very powerful all the same, as this case shows.

LOBBYING THE WRONG PERSON

A company wanted to build a chemical plant in a highly sensitive area. The authority which would give permission for this was at county council level. Naturally, the company set about wooing the local county councillor, a Mr Johnson, who was a member of the Liberal Democrat party.

He attended a site visit meeting with other councillors and seemed outwardly non-committal, but was probably antagonistic about the project.

LOBBYING THE WRONG PERSON *(cont'd)*

The company was briefing us on another project and mentioned this *en passant*. Our curiosity roused, we did a little investigation and undertook a mini-diagnostic. First, we found that the Liberal Democrats were not in power at county level, it was the Conservatives.

Second, from a cursory perusal of the company's correspondence with local people, it seemed that the district councillor, Mrs Smith, was running a major campaign against the project. She was a Conservative. The question now was: How much power will the district councillor have over her colleagues who serve on the county council?

Third, Mr Johnson's power base was not in the area where the plant was proposed at all. (County councillors cover a much wider area than district councillors: in fact there were four district councils within the county councillor's area.) Mr Johnson's areas of support were in other districts. This explained his lack of real concern. However, he had nothing to lose by opposing the project, so would do so.

Finally, Mr Johnson was not the key player: his party was not in power. In effect, the company was trying to influence the wrong person.

Analysis
This had a number of implications:

1. By missing out the district councillor, Mrs Smith, the company was missing out on a key player who could probably either make or break the project.
2. By ignoring (as she would see it) Mrs Smith, they were further entrenching her in her antagonistic position.
3. The company looked like they did not know the local scene. This naïvety was translated into a lack of concern for local people.
4. Politicians like to deal with people who understand them and their drivers – this company was not showing this.

(Postscript: Following our intervention, contact was made with the district councillor; modifications were made to the plan – for which she took the credit – and the project proceeded.)

The outcome of this case was a win–win project (dealt with in detail in the next chapter), thanks to the intervention of a TPA who got something for her community. However, TPAs can remain hidden and, if not positively and properly motivated, can quickly turn into strong opponents.

Trade associations and think-tanks

In theory, an industry's trade association has the task of defending and promoting an industry on generic issues. In effect, it should act like a TPA. But while trade associations have real and valid roles on a number of fronts, they are hampered in being TPAs by a number of factors.

The 'who's paying the piper' effect
Because the association is directly funded by an industry, it is perceived to have a lack of independence. 'They would say that, wouldn't they', is the response. However, now it is even stronger: 'They have to say that, don't they?' This weakens the effectiveness of their efforts. In fact, as trade associations are even more distant from the organisation, they have less credibility. They are too often seen as puppets in the hands of their paymasters.

Preoccupation with vocal opponents
As the trade association has been founded with the sole aim of defending and promoting an industry, it should be first into battle when that industry is attacked. It should rebuff every attack and win every battle. Unfortunately, this tends to distract the association and considerable resources can be expended on single-issue pressure groups, which, as we saw earlier, is a total waste of time. As before, this has two detrimental effects: (a) the small group gets increased credibility now that the industry is 'taking it seriously', and (b) other work goes undone – particularly that of forming alliances. (Ironically, trade associations are often urged on by their members to tackle these groups in the mistaken belief that it will remove pressure from individual members.)

Trade association structure
In general, trade associations tend to have large numbers of committees with many members. One trade association has 15 committees and sub-committees with up to 20 members on each. The reasons for this are to give some sort of role to every member – to keep them happy – but there are a number of detrimental outcomes:

- *Time constraints.* All the company representatives have busy and responsible jobs so the amount of time they give to the trade association tends to be small. It is not unusual for members to read their papers in the taxi on the way to a meeting and then not consider the association until the next meeting in a month's time.

■ *Lack of management.* With such a loose structure, the full-time executive of the trade association has a reasonably free hand. However, with a multitude of members, they often seek refuge in covering their own backsides and a culture of risk aversion soon builds up, which in effect makes the organisation ineffective.

■ *Lack of focus.* With so many members, no clear voice comes through and the association tries to be all things to all men. The association tries to take on too many tasks with the result that it does none well.

■ *Dominance by one player.* Out of the chaos, one member company tries to impose its will on the organisation and appoints a senior figure to give more time to it. This inevitably fails as other companies resent this 'takeover bid' and stop co-operating or, indeed, begin actively to hinder.

■ *The 'whatever will we do with George' syndrome.* Often, trade associations are dumping grounds (harsh words, but true) for executives who are on the way out of an organisation. However, the company does not want to be so cruel as to throw them immediately on the scrap heap so they are asked 'to bring their considerable management experience to bear' on the trade association, through a secondment or some such placement. George, unfortunately, is a chemical or mechanical engineer with no knowledge of communications. But that doesn't matter, it's all just common sense, isn't it? True, but so is building a nuclear power plant and we don't see many communications managers in charge of that.

Think-tanks
From these points, it will be obvious that some other form of organisation is necessary. Ideally, this organisation should have some of the following qualities:

■ *Independence.* The organisation must be seen to be independent. This gives credibility and helps differentiate the organisation from the industry.

■ *Respected.* The organisation should be well established, so that it can 'hit the ground running', rather than have to build its credentials which can take many years, if not decades.

■ *Research capability.* The organisation should have enough research clout to be taken seriously at the highest levels.

■ *Freedom.* It cannot be seen to be fettered by the industry.

■ *Public profile*. The organisation must have the ability to speak out without fear. For example, it must have the ability to be controversial and thought provoking.

The type of organisation which meets all of these criteria is a think-tank. These are widely used in politics and most have strong affiliations with their political masters – yet they are seen as independent. Universities and their research capabilities are widely used by the green groups. Their ideal home is often within a university or learned institutional body. An industry think-tank has a number of advantages:

■ *Independence*. It should be truly independent and left to its own devices; otherwise it is just a trade association. By being so, it fulfils one of the key attributes of a third party advocate. Also, this independence will lead to some minor criticisms of the industry, but that – we noted earlier – is healthy and leads to greater credibility. Enough controls should be in place to ensure that the think-tank does not go off the rails and launch widespread attacks on its sponsoring industry.

■ *Media credibility*. Media seldom look closely at the ancestry of think-tanks and tend to have a much higher acceptance of their utterances than those which come directly from industry or the trade association.

■ *Political credibility*. A think-tank can provide a useful neutral meeting ground for politicians to meet an industry. They can host many of these events.

The role of employees

Too often, with the huge emphasis on centralised communications programmes, employees are forgotten as third party advocates. This does not mean the slick company spokesperson with a 30-second sound-bite ready for TV. No, it is real 'live' employees who do not spout the company line who make first-class and highly credible advocates. These people are believed – they are real, they have not been briefed, they don't have a carefully prepared sound bite, or a carefully prepared 'question and answer' sheet, with lots of questions but few answers, up their sleeve.

However, most large corporations have a policy of threatening all employees with dismissal if they should speak to the press. Why is this? Do they not trust the employees? The answer, unfortunately, is 'yes'. And how do the employees react to this lack of trust? They feel rejected. So there are two detrimental results:

- strong potential advocates of the company are muzzled
- the lack of trust by the employer is a huge incentive to leak or whistle-blow. Civil service departments are classic examples of this.

For larger organisations – with a number of sites – middle managers and supervisory staff on the ground can be powerful spokespersons. Certainly, they will suffer a little from having a vested interest in protecting their jobs – but they have real credibility as the workers at the coalface rather than the faceless public relations executive from corporate HQ. They should be involved early in any contentious project.

Conclusion

Third party advocates can have a powerful influence on a project – in effect, they can most times either make or break it. However, they are of little use unless they take action and this is the subject of the next chapter.

10

Getting TPAs to Act on a Project

From the stakeholder audit, the diagnostic and other work, it will become clear that there are perhaps three or four people who might have an interest in the project on which we are working. Often, they are politicians, ward councillors and the like. Often, they are local luminaries, for example in the civic society. Seldom are they the local pressure or environmental groups.

How to approach people

Such are the social niceties of our modern civilised society that it is increasingly difficult for us to approach people we do not know. This is particularly so when we are in – or about to enter – a conflictual situation. Rare is the manager who relishes a work performance review with a staff member who is operating below par.

But until people can actually sit down and face each other then progress is not possible. Even in the most entrenched position, there is always some flexibility. But to unearth this flexibility, a dialogue must commence. The situation in Northern Ireland and in the Middle East (both of which will, no doubt, have moved on since this book was written) are prime examples. Yet with the use of mediation and goodwill on both sides, the levels of mistrust can be reduced so that a dialogue can begin. Neither side is ever completely happy. This is natural – both have had to give away a little of their position.

These are some of the reasons why a dialogue does not occur:

- *Labelling*. From a great distance, we decide that someone is an enemy. This may be because of a quote in a newspaper article, because of some

107

piece of hearsay or just because that is how we think that person should be. So we decide that all socialists are anti-business, that all conservatives are anti-trades unions, that all residents are anti-development and that all politicians are cynical. Nothing is further from the truth. Political parties are broad churches and, within any grouping of people, each individual will hold individual views. These often run counter to those of the majority in that grouping.

- *Fear*. We do not like conflict so we avoid it. How will we react – in a one-to-one highly personal situation – with this person who we believe hates us. Do we shake hands or is that premature? Who sits down first? All of these thoughts – very human as they are – stop us making the first move.

- *It's never been done before*. Most things that are really worthwhile have never been done before. The fear of learning is a huge one and when faced with the challenge, we tend to revert to behaviour we are more familiar with. In controversial environmental projects, it is far easier to send out a press release on a Friday evening from the comfort of one's desk rather than arrange to meet a local politician on a Sunday morning.

- *It's too risky*. A cousin of the last reason – but now we justify our fear with a vague threat that the whole project may be threatened, as this example shows.

THE NEW INCINERATOR

A regional local authority had decided that an incinerator was its only way of dealing with waste. As with many authorities nowadays, it decided to utilise a private company to undertake the construction and management of this enterprise.

We were surveying the local media on behalf of another client and we noticed that this was the big local hot issue. Both the local members of parliament (from different parties) had mounted campaigns; the local newspaper had organised a petition and the local district councils were up in arms lest this menace be sited in their areas.

After we finished our work for our original client, we called the private waste company to see if we could be of any service. The response was astonishing. 'I am amazed that you believe there are any public relations problems. Everything is under control, said the director of communications. We pointed to the opposition locally. He angrily riposted: 'Yes, but we have a road show and major media

---

THE NEW INCINERATOR *(cont'd)*

---

campaign starting next month and this will bring the truth out. We haven't even begun to talk facts yet – but when we present the facts, then you will see a huge change. The politicians will run out of steam and then they will come around.'

We never got to work for that potential client and the incinerator has still to be built.

■ *We don't want to be accused of lobbying.* This is a very legitimate reason – lobbying is rapidly becoming a disgraced art. In many countries, there are now – rightly – strong laws governing lobbying.

However, consulting with local people, understanding their needs and reacting to them is not lobbying – it is consultation. Something which is enshrined in all modern democracies.

The first approach

By even approaching these people, cover will have been broken. Organisations are hugely sensitive about this: what happens if they go to the media? What happens if they form an action group? If these things are going to happen, then they are going to happen anyway.

When approached, it is highly likely that the person will tell someone else. So, for example, if one approaches the chairman of the parish council, he or she will tell the clerk or other members what is happening. On occasion, he or she may not, but it is as well to assume that the mere fact of approaching someone is telling them that something major is about to happen.

We will not necessarily be made aware of these discussions – this is normal. As we saw from the interplay within the power pyramid, it will not take long for our intervention to become common knowledge. As far as the key movers and shakers in the community are concerned, we might as well have taken out an advertisement in the local paper.

However, if we have undertaken our diagnostic correctly, we will not have breached protocol. In particular, we have not gone prematurely public (the DAD strategy). There will be curiosity to see where we are coming from. And there should be a certain relief for the politicians in particular that we decided to take some soundings on the ground before going for a full-scale public launch.

The diagnostic has a second important role now. It allows us to talk to people at the minutest level on their terms. This is important. Too often projects are launched with only a cursory knowledge of the locality. Not only is this dangerous (one can only guess at what land-mines one is walking on) but it is insulting. The politician who has to ask: 'But surely you know the local hospital is closing?' will not have much respect for the organisation that does not know this key fact. It also shows a lack of care and concern for the community. It says: 'All we really want to do is get in here, get our project finished, make a profit and get out.' These early signals are very difficult to retract.

Finally, the diagnostic allows one to open a conversation on familiar ground for both parties. This chit chat is normal social human behaviour. Jumping straight into the business in hand is, in most cultures, discourteous.

After the initial attunement, it is important that questions are kept on a general level. Broad, open questions are best; for example:

- What do you know about the project?
- What do you think of the project? (the answer can be very hurtful)
- What would make the project better?
- Who else should we talk to?

The answers to these simple questions are most revealing, not so much on what people know, but rather on the level of *lack* of knowledge. In one case, a councillor said: 'I have not read any of the documents pertaining to this project – I don't need to: I know it is bad and I will oppose it totally.' It was the same councillor who later said: 'You know I have now read the original document – it wasn't that bad at all.' One should not attempt to correct facts at this stage – there will be plenty of time for people to come to their own realisation of the facts in due course.

Neither is the objective to lobby, it is to ascertain levels of knowledge, but more important, to find out what the problems with the project are and what might make it better, so as to make it acceptable.

In general, interviews should last about one hour or longer in order to be assured that true views – not just superficial knee jerks – are being given.

These first interviews should ascertain the positions of the people concerned. They should also begin to give an indication as to who are the really useful TPAs rather than those we *think* are useful.

They may suggest initiatives which might be taken:

■ *Modifications to the proposals.* This is the biggest fear of organisations. 'If we open this up to every Tom, Dick and Harry', they say, 'they will make totally unreasonable demands on us. They will change the project totally and it will be unworkable'. Nothing is further from the truth. For the most part, we are dealing with supporters. The intractable opponents are being ignored (politely, of course). Those approached are people who may want the project to succeed.

In our experience, the modifications demanded are small and generally involve very local issues: traffic control around the entrance to a site, for example. In addition, non-technical people do not have the technical ability to make radical changes: long way around in technical projects, we are all in the hands of the engineers and the scientists.

■ *Other TPAs.* There should be a review of who the potential TPAs, supporters and opponents may be. It will be remarkable how these views differ from our first stakeholder audit. People who were labelled as total opponents are being touted by people on the ground as potential supporters.

■ *Win–win projects.* These are one of the most important outputs from these meetings and are dealt with in the next section.

Win–win projects

These are sometimes within the scope of the project, but sometimes have nothing at all to do with it. Examples we have encountered include the case of the creation of the new community centre seen in an earlier chapter, a new bus halting area for the school bus (as the old one was potentially dangerous) or a new notice board for the residents' association.

What these projects have in common is that the demands are not exorbitant. They are small improvements that will make a substantial improvement in a community. Yet they are often overlooked: negotiations are conducted almost totally between the technical experts on both sides. The local people and their representatives are often bypassed: is it little wonder they often oppose – there is nothing in the project for them.

However, too often organisations tend to expect communities to accept a project on a win–lose basis. Or even worse on a win–win basis, where they define both sides of the deal: they decide what they get and they also decide what the community gets, as this case shows.

THE SUNDAY MARKET

A company wanted to build a major new hypermarket, with shops and restaurants in a city centre area. The local council (especially its planners) was very much in favour of the idea, as it was part of their urban regeneration programme. The area was previously occupied by a factory – which had been cleared – but the site was still a bit of an eyesore.

Naturally, with a major project like this, there was going to be a large car park. The town had a problem: it was about to lose the area where the traditional Sunday market was held (again due to urban regeneration) and the planners and the developers thought it might be a good idea to have the market (which took place in the morning) in the new car park. It was a neat solution, killing two birds with one stone. However, the difference between this and shooting oneself in both feet simultaneously is small.

When the plans were announced, the local residents, especially those nearest the proposed hypermarket, were up in arms. This was expected. Although the old factory site was a bit of an eyesore, it was just open ground. They were not overlooked, neither did it generate any traffic in the area.

But what was not expected was the backlash against the market. These middle-class people did not want a market which they thought (although they never said this) would attract bargain hunters and bring in hundreds of extra cars to their area. The company and the planners thought they were doing the town a favour, but the opposite was the case. Again, the local residents were in favour of a market – but not in their backyard.

The moral of this story is that one must be careful in imposing projects on a community, even if those projects seem to bring a benefit. Think of the difficulty one has in choosing a gift for a loved one, someone one knows well, perhaps whom you have lived with all your life. It's not easy. Now think of trying to buy a gift for someone you have never met, about whom you know very little. Will the gift be well received? An inappropriate gift will certainly look like a bribe or worse.

It is far better that local benefits are defined locally, as the following case shows.

THE NEW HOUSING DEVELOPMENT

Although new housing developments can be contentious, particularly in built-up areas, there is an acceptance that new homes are needed and must be built. In the UK, areas for new housing are allocated in local plans, after widespread consultation.

The Shannon Bay site has been in the local plan for ten years, so the fact that housing was to be built there was no surprise to anyone. It was to be a big estate with 1,400 houses built over a number of years.

The company promoting the site was going about business in the usual manner, holding public meetings, talking to the media, organising a site visit for members of the council and negotiating with the officers of the council. The project was looking good politically. Although the council was hung, the project had the support of the two major parties as well as the leaders of the council. In addition, officers said that – despite the difficult politics – the scheme was safe.

There were a number of substantial gains for the community in the scheme:

- a major new park area would be donated by the company – this would host a number of playing fields
- an acre of land would be given to the community for its own uses
- a gift of £25,000 would be given to the existing community centre.

The council meeting came and, to everyone's surprise, the planning application was rejected by 27 votes to 25. Three of the Liberal councillors had defied their party whip and voted with the opposition. These three members were all local to the site and felt there was a strong groundswell of opinion against the scheme. The problems as they saw them were:

- the scheme was too big
- it would exacerbate existing traffic problems
- the schools were full
- the medical centre was under pressure.

All of these issues had been aired previously and there were perfectly rational answers:

- the scheme was the same size it had always been
- the company was to build a new access road
- the schools were not full
- the medical centre was – according to the local authority – coping well.

When we went to work on the project, we conducted a diagnostic. It was obvious that, given the delicate state of the politics in the council, it would need cross-party

THE NEW HOUSING DEVELOPMENT *(cont'd)*

support in order for the project to be approved. In other words, the Liberals, Conservatives and Labour parties would have to support it.

This was the state of the parties:

Liberals   28
Conservatives   12
Labour   12

The Liberals were vulnerable at the next election and both the Conservatives and the Labour group were anxious to take advantage of this. Both were running full-blooded opposition and were eyeing each other like hawks.

The Liberals were likely to split on this issue given the strength – as the local members saw it – of local feeling. Therefore cross-party support was needed.

After our work on the diagnostic, we began a stakeholder audit. A key figure to emerge from this was the chairman of the community association. Despite the enticements of an acre of land and the substantial grant of £25,000 the association was still opposing the development.

We went to speak to her and also began a dialogue with some of the local politicians. The chairman of the community association was surprised at our phone call and readily agreed to meet. She started by explaining the history of the organisation – of which we were aware – and then outlined its expansion plans: they wanted to add a new sports centre. Certainly the gift of £25,000 from the company was useful, but not necessary (this was a surprise), as they already had substantial funds in the bank.

She then went and got a drawing of the new sports facilities. I asked where these might go and she said they would go opposite the existing centre. However, if the acre of land being granted by the company was placed anywhere else other than opposite the existing centre their plans would fail. So if the acre of land were locked into that specific location, would they support? Yes, with one other condition, that the acre be released immediately rather than when the 500th house was built.

We went back to the company and they were shocked. Was that all? Yes, but these factors were hugely important to the community centre and would allow it to get on with its plans. More significantly, one of the local councillors was on the committee of the centre and he had voted against.

We then spoke to the local politicians and their fears were as they had outlined, but there was more. The new sports fields were far from the older existing housing development. Parents were anxious about sending their young children so far away.

THE NEW HOUSING DEVELOPMENT *(cont'd)*

Again, we looked at the scheme and found that an 'urban park' – a large area of open land within the site – could be used to house a junior sports field and this could be moved (everything is possible on a CAD screen) to be near the existing development. This made the local representative very happy, although he still vowed he would vote against the scheme.

As our negotiations continued, other minor areas of flexibility were negotiated and granted. What was interesting was that the total cost of all the changes was very small in the context of the total scheme.

The Conservative and Labour groups claimed credit for some of the changes and between them agreed they would support the scheme next time round. The Liberals said that the original scheme was good but that the new scheme was better so they would again support it.

On the night, the vote was 49 for to 3 against – the local councillors remained faithful to those who they represented and who had elected them. Rightly so – that is democracy.

Like St Paul on the road to Damascus, those who come from one side of the fence to the other are truly powerful advocates. With the zeal of the reformed harlot (with no disrespect to the many TPAs we have worked with) they will fight like no other for their project. They may adopt a number of roles which may seem surprising to many corporations:

- They may be asked to take part in a meeting of the steering group.
- They may be asked to become part of the steering group if their enthusiasm is strong enough.
- They may form another organisation with other people who have met them.
- They may have an existing organisation which can act as a platform for their work.
- Things we have not yet thought of – there are always surprises.

Of course, this means a huge trust in people. But as humans, although we have our unpleasant side, most of us are – for the most part – honest. We don't steal from supermarket shelves, even though the produce is readily available, we don't drive away from service station forecourts without paying. It is not the fear of punishment – it is because we are honest – it is part of our ethics.

This initial interview allows one to categorise people and to be fairly sure that the categorisation is correct. This is particularly so when defining those who are against a project: are we sure that the opposition is real and, more importantly, total? Or is it that they just oppose one aspect of the project? It is nearly always the latter, unless they are part of that intractably opposed pressure group.

The use of a mediator

This phase – of directly approaching people – is one which is always difficult for organisations. They ask: How do I go about meeting someone I don't know? What will I say to them? What if I am rebuffed? (None of us likes rejection so this question is seldom verbalised.) What if a mob turns up to the meeting? And many more.

As human beings, we are, for the most part, shy and reticent creatures. We are carefully nurtured in our social structures of what does and does not constitute acceptable behaviour.

Certainly, approaching outright strangers in the street is not acceptable in most societies. This is particularly so if we are in, or about to enter, a conflictual situation with them. Of course, it is not easy to approach someone and say: 'Hi, I would like to build an incinerator in your back yard if that's OK.'

No, it is much safer to hide and to make the announcement in the traditional way – the DAD approach.

However, there is an easier solution – the use of a mediator. In fact, as well as saving an organisation the angst of a difficult meeting, the mediator will have a more fruitful dialogue.

The use of mediators on the world stage is well accepted. In the 1970s, Henry Kissinger invented shuttle diplomacy as he tried to broker an agreement between Israel and the Arab states. In Northern Ireland, Senator George Mitchell plied back and forth between the opposing sides trying to find middle ground.

In both cases, there are some common elements:

1. Neither side will talk to the other, however they will talk to the intermediary.

2. The intermediary must be personable and not only willing to listen, but also to show that they have listened. It is certainly not the place for people with 'spiky' personalities as this just opens up another conflict.

3. They must be reasonably agenda-free, although neutrality is not a major issue (even though in an ideal world it helps). Certainly, no-one could accuse Senator Mitchell of having any 'baggage', but Henry Kissinger was Jewish and none the less effective.

4. They must present as seeking to consult without any fixed ideas on the outcome. This is very important. If the intermediary acts as a lobbyist, the project is finished.

5. The company must be willing to listen to the concessions required and be flexible in their response to them. This is also essential: an intermediary without some flexibility and room to manoeuvre is like a poker player without chips.

   Certainly, companies can be reluctant to use intermediaries, particularly those firms with a strong control fixation. The attitude is: why can't we do this in-house? Can we really trust this person? What if they give too much away?

The advantages of an intermediary

Compared to a company employee or a professional lobbyist, an intermediary brings a number of advantages:

1. Independence – although this may seem surprising, intermediaries – even when paid for by one side – are seen as independent, particularly after the initial suspicions have worn off. And so they not only should, but MUST be. (In fact, the hiring company will often go through a phase of thinking the intermediary has gone native and is now working for the other side.)

2. The ability to negotiate without any negotiating power. If the two opposing sides sit down together, each knows that the other is in a position to come to an agreement there and then. This leads to friction and to people upping their demands artificially to get a better bargaining position. The result is often that the chasm between the sides increases rather than decreases: antagonism is increased and the meeting ends not only in failure, but also an even deeper division with further loss of trust. A mediator can put various scenarios forward, always in the knowledge that they will have to be brought back to the other side. In fact, the mediator can propose solutions that either side would not

countenance. They can think the unthinkable and say it, without loss of face or the increasing of tension.

3. Finding the real (and usually hidden) agendas and getting true views. People will talk much more openly to a third party. They can then launch an oblique attack, often using phrases such as; 'If the managing director of that company was in this room right now, I would tell him what a right mess his company is making of this project. Does he know, for example, that his employees break every noise regulation in the book', and so on. This sort of direct dialogue is much more difficult when the actual opponents are face to face. Of course, one gets vitriol at a public meeting, but seldom do the real agendas come out then. For example, people may complain about traffic from a new factory, but, in public, they will seldom talk about the potential detrimental effects on their house prices. This is often the real agenda. However, to talk about this in public looks like greed and selfishness, so remains hidden.

4. Finding the conditions people have for accepting a proposal. These are always surprising. They are generally not onerous and often easily met. Second, they are never exactly what one expects at the beginning. There are always surprises. If these surprises are not unearthed, then they fester and become time bombs, which will explode at some stage.

Conclusion

As human beings we only have written and verbal communications at our disposal. It is amazing how much more content large organisations are with the former. Yet it is the latter that brings true results.

Part IV
Communication Tools

11 The Use and Limitations of Traditional Marketing-led Mass Communication Techniques

Unless properly used – with correct timing – all written and broadcast communications, market research, advertising, brochures, press releases and the like, are potentially very dangerous in issues management. They need to be used with care.

Traditional marketing and public relations techniques

For almost every organisation, some form of formal marketing or communications function is an essential part of the business structure. This applies to government and public sector bodies as well as profit-making companies. Marketing – in particular, advertising – has been spectacularly successful.

Intrinsic to all these techniques is an assumption that the customer either wants the product on offer or can be persuaded to develop a desire for it. Certainly, over the years marketing has evolved from being product led, where the company made a gizmo and hoped someone would buy it. Then there was the marketing-led approach where research showed gaps in the market. The latest techniques feature market driving – finding new ways to drive the customer towards the product. The new Internet shops are examples of this: if you buy a product once, a record or a book for example, you will be made offerings in the same vein as they come along.

Given the common ancestry of both disciplines – how to get mentioned in the newspapers – it is not surprising that both marketing and PR, often seen as a branch of the former discipline, continue to use very similar techniques.

A COMMON ANCESTRY – ADVERTISING AND PUBLIC RELATIONS

Although communications and marketing are getting increasingly sophisticated the basic principles have hardly altered in 100 years. If we look back to that simpler time, the few forms of mass communication included:

- displays of various kinds, posters and shop windows, for example
- public meetings, exhibitions, and so on
- flyers through letter boxes – as popular then as they are now
- newspapers
- word of mouth, gossip, if you will.

However, despite the sophistication of modern communications methods and marketing strategies, little has really changed. The various displays – shop windows and the like – are still with us and, until recently, the retail giant Marks & Spencer involved itself in almost no advertising except its shop frontages. It is interesting also that the whole area of what is now known as marketing evolved from this. The Irish Marketing Society can trace its lineage to an organisation for window displays.

Certainly, we have displays of various kinds (the poster industry has never been more ubiquitous) and there are vast arenas devoted to exhibitions for goods as diverse as cars to underwear. Although public meetings are on the wane and the days of the old barnstorming political rally are not what they were, they still have a powerful force, thanks mainly to television which can bring the meeting to thousands of people. We still get numerous flyers – often in the form of free newspapers – through our letterboxes.

However, if we go back 100 years, there was no mass radio, no TV, no satellites, no Internet. The only means of mass communication was the newspaper. Both government and commerce saw the potential of newspapers to influence people. The former was afraid and the latter excited. Indeed, when radio and TV came along, the first instinct of governments – in Europe, at any rate – was to bring them under state control. For the British Broadcasting Corporation, this meant no advertising. In fact, the mention of any proprietary brand name on the BBC was taboo until recently. On the continent, advertising was heavily restricted – lest, no doubt, it might somehow corrupt the minds of those that might see or hear it.

Therefore, as a means of true mass communication, that left newspapers as the only real outlet. In effect, 100 years ago, it was the main marketing tool available to those who wished to sell their wares. There were two ways of getting a mention in the newspaper – either you paid by advertising or you got a mention in an article. Immediately, it became apparent that the latter was far more powerful than the former as it had the authority of a third party advocate – the independent newspaper – behind

A COMMON ANCESTRY – ADVERTISING AND PUBLIC RELATIONS *(cont'd)*

it. From advertising grew the discipline of marketing and, in parallel, public relations, or more correctly, media relations, was born. It was ideal: cheap (on the surface, almost free) publicity, which was more powerful than advertising which was expensive. So organisations had a 'press officer', not a public relations manager.

However, newspaper editors were not stupid, and they realised that if they fed their readers PR pap, they would soon lose their own credibility, so they were quick to filter out the PR industry's efforts. Often, they would turn the attempted press relations effort on its head and make a negative story. The problem with media relations was that, like a rugby ball in the air, there was no guarantee as to how it would bounce or where it would land.

Companies soon realised that, if they wanted guaranteed results and a consistent message, the most effective way to achieve this was to advertise. To this day, advertising is dominant over public relations in terms of budgets and effect. If a firm wants to increase sales by 10 per cent, then it knows that the most reliable way to do this is by advertising – with PR in a much lower ranking subsidiary role. (There are, of course, exceptions, such as the Body Shop.)

Despite the efforts of many PR professionals, this system exists almost to the present day: public relations is still the poor cousin of advertising. As the section on evaluation will show, there is still a misguided fascination with column inches: the industry has hardly moved on from the days of the press officer. But hard-nosed business people and, increasingly, government organisations, want results. Advertising can deliver – PR is still in many respects an unknown quantity.

So when a company wants to communicate, it tends to reach instinctively for the tried and trusted communications mechanisms: advertising, press relations, brochures, direct mail, and so on. But, when dealing with controversial issues, the problem is that the customer has no desire to have the product and, in fact, often finds it quite repugnant. However, companies continue to use the techniques of marketing and public relations.

The attractions of traditional communications techniques

The traditional communications methods are advertising, press releases, public meetings, notices on boards and the like. A central message is crafted and then it is broadcast to everyone.

The overt advantages of mass communications are fairly obvious.

Control

Organisations – and particularly large corporations – like to control what they refer to as their image, brand or brand values. So, for example, Shell has many large volumes of guidance devoted to its corporate identity – in effect, how you can use and not use the logo. Not that Greenpeace pays much attention to that.

Similarly, the PR department likes to control the tone of voice the company uses in its public statements. For commercial firms in competitive marketplaces, this consistency is very important in the company's marketing plans. Dissonant or inconsistent messages can confuse the consumer and damage sales. So, there is a strong control fixation within organisations.

All of the traditional methods of communication easily satisfy this need. In the comfort of one's office, one can carefully titivate advertisements or press releases. They can be then passed to colleagues who can do the same until a consistent message is honed.

Resources

When a company needs to communicate with an outside audience, it looks to its own resources. This is hardly surprising. After all, the organisation's human resources director has convinced the board that they 'only hire the best and reward them accordingly'. The annual report has stated, yet again, that the company's biggest asset is its people. (Although why this thought is usually left to the last paragraph of the chairman's statement is a bit of an oxymoron.)

Most companies have the resources either in-house or through agencies to produce these mass communications. And because these resources are located centrally, this is an immediate bias towards crafting one central message. Budgets have been allocated to do this work, so again there is a strong incentive to do it in this fashion.

Cost

Although mechanisms like advertising seem expensive, they are a particularly cheap way of getting to thousands of people quickly and efficiently with one message. Press releases – after they are written – only cost a stamp and a piece of paper.

So, for the large organisation, mass communication mechanisms are highly attractive. They offer control, resources for them exist and they certainly look cost effective.

Problems with mass communications

There is no doubt that advertising works. Just open your newspaper or watch the television. It's heaving with advertising. And it has been for years. If advertising did not work, companies would not have continued with it. And the industry has got increasingly sophisticated in its ability to measure how effective certain advertisements are with certain audiences. Gone are the days when Lord Bourneville said: 'I know half of my advertising is effective, but I do not know which half.'

So with a contentious issue, why not simply advertise your way out of trouble? Throw money at it with big, strong, powerful messages. The reasons are many and they apply to almost all means of mass communications. But there are real problems when these mechanisms are applied to contentious or difficult issues – when the customer does not want to buy and finds the product offensive.

Scepticism

In classical marketing, some of the consumers have a desire and a need for the product or service; they are open to communications about the product and – because they have an unfulfilled need – they are willing to begin to believe the communications message. Certainly, they may have some scepticism of the claims made by the organisation making the offer, but still they are willing potential buyers.

Unfortunately, in contentious issues, there are very few willing buyers. And because there is not an unfulfilled need, people tend not to believe the mass communications mechanisms. The scepticism noted earlier becomes outright disbelief and the communication is either ignored or, and this is common, it arouses anger and cements people further into their opposition.

PRIVATISING THE WATER INDUSTRY

In the mid-1980s, the UK's privatisation programme was in full flow. The state was busy divesting itself of almost everything. After an astute campaign by the water industry – led in particular by Thames Water chairman Roy Watts (later Sir Roy) – that industry got to the head of the queue for the auction rooms.

This was to prove the most unpopular privatisation ever. First, people did not understand why a monopoly should be privatised. Unlike, say, British Airways, or to a

---

PRIVATISING THE WATER INDUSTRY *(cont'd)*

---

lesser extent, British Telecom that were in competitive markets, water was a fairly tightly sealed monopoly.

Second – it was the stuff of life. Humans can go without food for weeks – as hunger strikers prove, but we will die after only a few days without water. Could such an essential element be trusted to the forces of the market?

Then the green groups got in on the act and started to spread horror stories about pesticides, aluminium, nitrates and other substances in tap water, which also had the secondary effect of doing wonders for the sales of bottled water.

Finally, in a series of well-aimed shots to the foot, the industry had a number of crises in the run-up to the privatisation. A parasite called cryptosporidium was found in water in Oxford, huge amounts of aluminium sulphate were pumped into water in Cornwall and during the summer there were the usual problems with supply – the dreaded hosepipe bans.

As the industry was a monopoly, it had never embarked on any major marketing campaigns. The companies had press offices, but what was the point of a marketing campaign? Nearly all customers were on fixed tariffs – metering was still rare in the UK – so there was little advantage encouraging them to use more water, especially as there was none to spare. Conversely, many of the advertising campaigns were counselling restraint, particularly in the summer.

However, those in the City now demanded that the industry raise its profile and begin to market itself so as to hype up the market for shares. Suddenly, there were major advertising campaigns on the television and in the press extolling the virtues of the water companies and what a fine job they were doing.

This campaign was greeted first with derision and then anger. People's perception of the water industry was one of quiet workmanship. They did not want to think about it. They turned on the taps and the water came out. They did not see this as rocket science. They certainly did not want their intelligence insulted by being told that what they saw as the dozy old water company was suddenly some bright modern public limited company like IBM.

The anger was engendered by the simple question of: Who is paying for all this fancy advertising? The water consumers, that was who. This angered people enormously, mainly because the water charge was seen as a form of taxation – in reality, it was known as water rates. People thought: why don't they reduce the cost instead?

Finally, people did not believe the messages, given the backdrop of disasters that the industry was inflicting on itself.

PRIVATISING THE WATER INDUSTRY *(cont'd)*

As well as privatisation being a contentious issue, the industry was now faced with a second problem: the advertising itself had become an issue. There were letters to the newspapers, politicians put down questions in the House of Commons, and customers were writing threatening to withhold that part of their rates which was devoted to advertising.

Despite all this, the industry was privatised in 1989, not because of the advertising campaign, but due to the resilience of Mrs Thatcher and a large majority – coupled with the fact that the next election was not until 1992.

Analysis

Ironically, it could be argued that the advertising campaign had almost the exact opposite effect it was designed to have: instead of promoting the industry, it damaged it.

So, mass communication has to be handled very carefully in a sensitive issue. Other organisations in difficult industries have found similar problems.

The sin of origin

People have a natural filter by which they view all messages – this filter is scepticism. For example, in car retailing, all the advertisement can do is get the consumer into the showroom – it is the rare individual who orders direct from the advertisement. (Of course, there are exceptions with low-cost purchases (such as clothing) where the benefit is obvious and the risk is low, but these also give strong no-risk, money-back guarantees.) However, all mass communications messages are greeted with scepticism and when they involve a contentious issue, that scepticism can turn to cynicism or even anger as we have just seen. It can be neatly summed up by the immortal words of Mandy Rice-Davies, who was being questioned during the 1960s' court case on the Profumo scandal. She challenged the argument of a certain lord who claimed never to have met her by saying, 'Well, he would say that wouldn't he?' This neatly sums up the problem of company announcements, be they advertisements, press releases or leaflets.

The originator of the message is also the key difficulty facing the company spokesperson. These hapless souls are sent out to defend the most indefensible positions. People examine not only the message but also those who originated it. The effects are greatly reduced if the originator has something to gain by the message being believed.

People do not believe these spokespeople. Even if they are willing to give credibility to their position, it is tinged with huge levels of scepticism. People think that if you are paid to say something, then you will. With some justification. That is not to say that people lie, but they are putting the best possible spin on a situation. People, especially sceptical politicians and journalists, are well capable of filtering out the spin. Unfortunately, often much of what is left is (in the words of Henry Kissinger) 'content free'.

The green groups do not face the same problem. After all, they are independent guardians of the environment, who have nothing to gain personally, they are not corporate animals. They have no huge salaries to defend; they are taking on this role out of altruism. Aren't they? And their statements are never content free as they do not have to stick to the facts.

The written word

Organisations go to great lengths – not least because of the controls of regulatory bodies outlined earlier – to ensure that the statements they issue are accurate. Red pens and erasers abound as documents are carefully titivated and polished. This process can take many days. Eventually, there emerges a document that satisfies everyone, but usually at the same time satisfies no-one. The public relations manager thinks it is too weak and complex, the legal director thinks it is too risky and the technical director says it is too simplistic.

All documents – brochures, advertisements, press releases and so on – suffer from five major problems.

Documents are not read
The first problem is that – outside the company – almost no-one will read this document at all. There is too much information in the world – it is impossible to keep up with it – and this has been the case since long before the Internet.

Documents are scanned
And even if the document is read, it will not be read carefully with all the nuance and emphasis that have been built into it. Those carefully measured words, with 'would' changed to 'could' and then back again, are lost on the casual reader. They will scan headlines and quickly try to get the gist of what is in it. If they are familiar with the organisation (the sin of origin, again) and have preconceptions and prejudices about it, they will read the

---

THE WORST DOCUMENT I NEVER READ

A planning application had been rejected, although it could have brought huge benefits to a community. The officers of the council were – rightly – convinced that this was a superb deal. We were then employed by the organisation whose application had been rejected.

We began to talk to the politicians, including one of those who had voted against. Gently, we made an attempt to discern his level of knowledge of the planning application – a complex document of some 150 pages. He was very forthright and said: 'I have never read this application – I don't need to. My telephone is telling me what is in it.'

'What', he was asked, 'was the problem with the plans?' He said it was a bad application, which had little merit and would ruin the community. He then listed three major flaws. If, we asked, these were fixed, what would his attitude be? 'In that case,' he said, ' I could support this application – but there is no chance of major changes like that.'

This politician was working on totally erroneous information. Almost all the demands he had – and certainly the major ones – were already met. However, he could not be made to face this reality – it would be too hurtful. However, other cosmetic changes were made, the 'changes' he had wanted were reincorporated and he was very happy. The new application was very similar to the original. Afterwards, he approached us a little shame-facedly and said: 'Looking back at the original, it was not that bad after all. I am glad we got a second bite of the cherry.'

Analysis
Just because you have read a document does not mean that everyone else has – even though you might expect other people to have read it.

---

document through this filter. Documents from Monsanto suffer from this – we don't like GM foods and we don't like the people who are trying to influence us, therefore this document is a pack of lies, is the response.

People read what they think is written
The third problem follows on from this: it is that people read what they think the document says. This is especially true if it is reinforced by a green group selectively quoting or misquoting from it.

The memory gap
Finally, time erodes memories and eventually people think the document said something that was not in it.

Documents are final

However, the greatest and biggest danger with all documents is that once they are issued they can never be withdrawn. Circumstances may change, the world may change, but the document exists forever. And as someone once said, prediction is very difficult – especially about the future – so one should be very sure of one's ground before rushing into print.

The nuclear industry promised in the 1950s that electricity would be too cheap to meter. To this day, it is quoted back, even though circumstances have changed, the world has changed... the words of yesterday remain the words of today.

Qualified statements

Most marketing campaigns are successful when the organisation is able to make a strong, bold statement, for example, the classic from the UK retail chain – the John Lewis Partnership: 'Never knowingly undersold.' Certainly, it is a little quaint and old fashioned in its construction, but the message is clear. Similarly, there is no quibbling with BMW, 'the ultimate driving machine' or Carlsberg, 'Probably the best lager in the world'.

However, it should also be noted that each of these statements has a qualifier. For John Lewis it is 'knowingly' – the company is not promising the cheapest, it is promising that it will aspire to this. For BMW, the word 'ultimate' is subject to a number of interpretations and it would be possible to make the same claim for the Citroen 2CV or the Volkswagen Beetle. And, of course, Carlsberg's 'probably' is making an attribute of the qualifier, which is very clever.

Unfortunately, in the world of contentious issues, these strong, single statements can be very difficult to make. In fact, the qualifier becomes the source of contention. So with the mad cow disease debate, the government was not able to say 'absolutely no risk to human health' and the argument was lost to the law of the absolute. When dealing with issues like human health, food safety and the like, the word 'probably' has no place. So phrases such as 'probably the safest cut of beef in the world' reassures no-one. Or 'safety is never knowingly compromised' immediately begs the question: 'Why don't you find out.' This need to qualify strong statements leads to fudging and to weak, highly qualified statements.

In addition, the rules surrounding advertising are – rightly – very strong. In the UK, the Advertising Standards Authority insists that all advertising be 'decent, honest, legal and truthful'. Of course, any member of the public can object and their complaint will be reviewed by the Authority.

And this is a difficulty: one has to make a judgement on what is right and what is wrong. This is a human judgement and one that can be wrong. Equally, the ASA will make many claims, but infallibility is not one of them. The legal system does not always dispense justice – the ASA and similar organisations have the same problem.

Naturally, top of the list of scrutineers of all public utterances on contentious environmental issues will be the green groups. And being expert publicists, they take a number of bites at the cherry. First, when they decide to object to the advertisement, they will issue a press release where they will make outrageous claims about its content, saying that it is full of lies. This will inevitably be picked up by the media as it is a good conflictual story.

Then, when the result is announced, they will crow loudly (and rightly) on the few occasions when they are proved right. If their complaint is thrown out they will claim that it is all an establishment plot and that their claims – which will again be repeated by the media – were correct, whatever the regulator says.

Finally, they will continue to refer to their objection to the advertisement, often neglecting to mention that that objection failed to be upheld by the advertising authority.

Leaflets and direct mail

As well as suffering from all the problems associated with advertising and mass communication, letters, leaflets and other direct mail devices coming through people's doors have an additional problem: they can frighten people who have no reason (in many cases) to be concerned. So, when a letter arrives out of the blue, the question should be asked: 'How many other letters have people in this area received recently about a contentious project?' Probably none. That immediately positions the project as the most detrimental thing ever to happen in the area. These are some of the possible consequences:

- In reality, there are really only a small number of people who will be directly affected by the project. By involving many others – who only have a passing interest – it escalates the perceived impact of the project (ironically, those who you do not mail – outside the area – will probably say that they, too, are affected – by passing lorries or the like – and are being ignored).

- Some of these people will begin to contact their local politicians, who will be forced to take a position on the project. (See the next chapter on 'second-guessing the democratic system' for more on this.) As they are not thoroughly briefed, they have little choice but to show sympathy with their constituents' negative views. This may be reflected in the media. Later, it will be very difficult for them to 'unhook' themselves from this position. Politicians hate U-turns.

- By writing to 'members of the public' at roughly the same time as the politicians, this places them on a par. Yet politicians have trudged streets knocking on doors for votes, suffered abuse in so doing, and so on. They are the elected *representatives* of the people. Naturally, they expect different and preferential treatment. In addition, by 'going over their heads' to the electorate, they may feel bypassed and immediately become antagonistic.

- Naturally, politicians expect to be treated differently and to receive thorough and private briefings so that they can ask questions about the project. Privacy is essential, as some of the questions are often of the 'let me ask a stupid question' variety. This is very difficult to do in front of one's peers – especially from the opposition camp.

When are these techniques appropriate in environmental issues?

The answer is, as one would expect, a qualified one: probably never. If they are to be used they should either be authored or co-authored by a third party.

THE TRADES UNION BROCHURE

Nirex is the UK body charged with disposal of some the country's radioactive waste. The company has a difficult history and few friends. In the early 1990s the area chosen for a disposal site was near Sellafield in north-west England. It was also the site of the UK's biggest nuclear facility run by BNFL, which was also a major shareholder in Nirex.

BNFL's unions were powerful and the management of that company tended to work in a consensual way with them. However, the unions – for historical reasons – had had a difficult relationship with Nirex. Still, they were approached and after a number of meetings, a series of demands emerged from the union side. These

---

THE TRADES UNION BROCHURE *(cont'd)*

---

related to the future operation of the company in the area. After some negotiation, Nirex agreed to many of these demands.

After some time, the company decided to produce a brochure outlining its work in the community which, they felt, was substantial but unrecognised. When the union got wind of this, they volunteered to produce it instead. They interviewed local people and got local views.

Certainly, the brochure produced by the unions was very different from the one that the company intended to produce. It did not follow the party line and there were a number of statements that the company disagreed with. The company had relinquished rights to edit the brochure.

Analysis
The brochure was – in the strict view of the company – flawed, as it did not follow company policy. However, within it there was a ringing endorsement for the broad thrust of the work of the company. The endorsement was powerful for a number of reasons:

- It came from an independent third party which was well respected in the community and in the area.
- It came from a party which had previously been antagonistic to the company. This made it even more powerful. These people were not 'yes men and women', they were powerful scrutineers. They had extra credibility because of this.
- It was well received in the community and the media.

Conclusion

The techniques and methods of classical marketing are not easily adapted for controversial environmental projects. Certainly, they have a use, but that use is not in the early stages when the project is still in gestation and before people on the ground – particularly politicians – have had a chance to make their inputs.

12 Market Research: What do People Really Think and does it Matter?

One of my first encounters with market research was the most refreshing and also probably the most honest. I approached a professional in this field to undertake some research and his first question was: What results do you want? He was not joking. Market research – and associated exercises – find out what you want to know. It has never claimed that it can establish the truth in a particular situation.

Second-guessing the democratic system

There is a worrying trend by a number of people to try to find other ways to get around what they see as the rather tedious democratic system – they try to second-guess it. Even more seriously, there is a trend to take the results seriously as if they were a proper election poll.

It is all too easy to confuse democracy with the actual election and the announcement of results – it is much more than that. It is the run-up to election day, when the would-be representatives have to bring their manifestos to the people and try to convince them that theirs is the best way forward. This is an essential part of the democratic process and it is why instant elections are not allowed in real democracies.

So every four or five years, most politicians have to take to the streets, to be attacked by rabid dogs, to be seen kissing babies and to stand in the rain arguing with thoroughly unreasonable people who hate them. This is how they get elected. Anyone who has done this is very glad when it is all over. The people who get elected feel they have been through a rite of passage and are naturally proud that the people saw fit to entrust them to represent them. The elections over, they now want to get on with the business of governing.

What they do not want is to be running the election every other month. Yet that is what so many public consultation programmes are based upon: some method or other to second-guess the democratic system. These break into three main types:

- Market research – quantitative and qualitative
- Consensus conferences and citizens' juries
- Hands-on public consultation exercises of various kinds.

Market research – the dangers

In classical marketing, the first step is market research. Traditionally, this was undertaken to find out what demands there were in the marketplace for goods – it looked for gaps. So, in the 1950s, it would have been obvious that in Europe there was a huge unfilled market for electrical goods, from refrigerators to television sets.

Today, in the UK, almost everyone has a television and four out of five have a video recorder. Interestingly, the number of high earners with a VCR is almost the same as the number of low earners. So for the company which wants to sell VCRs today, it has to be far more sophisticated in its market research techniques, adding on extra features such as extra-fast rewind to satisfy an ever-demanding marketplace. But with increasingly sophisticated tastes and with demands for basic and luxury goods almost satisfied, companies are now seeking to drive the marketplace to whet people's appetites for goods.

The standard techniques are still in wide use: either quantitative market research – through surveys and the like – or the more sophisticated qualitative research through mechanisms like focus groups, which try to get to an extra layer of understanding. Both have problems when dealing with controversial projects.

Quantitative market research

This can be done by telephone, face-to-face or by written questionnaire. However, all these techniques face one fundamental obstacle: people do not tell the truth.

Take something as non-contentious as what we eat. In *Food in History* (revised edition, Penguin 1988) Reay Tannahill quotes a Euromonitor report which shows 63 per cent of people saying they increased their intake of fruit and vegetables, but mysteriously, market statistics had shown consumption had fallen by 10 per cent over the past five years. More interviewees said they were eating less meat, but meat consumption was way up.

She quotes another survey in Arizona where the researchers examined the contents of people's garbage cans after questioning them. They found that people ate '20 times more chocolate and 15 times more pastries than they had admitted in a consumer study. In Tucson, 85 per cent of people questioned said they did not drink beer – but 75 per cent of all dustbins inspected had beer cans in them.'

Perhaps Professor W. Rathje of the University of Arizona got it right when he said in the same source: 'Sift through dustbins if you want to know what people eat, they're more truthful than people.'

The reasons why people do not tell the truth are many and include:

- *The right answer.* From an early age in school, we are conditioned to give the right answer to questions. To give the wrong answer leads to either punishment or embarrassment. Therefore, we are conditioned to give the right answer, as to do otherwise makes us look stupid.

- *Protection of self-esteem.* We all have our internal pride and self-belief. We also want our privacy and are not willing to share intimate thoughts with absolute strangers. Therefore, we filter out the truth and give answers that are safe and do not betray or compromise our self-esteem.

- *Nothing to lose.* In quantitative market research, the interviewer and interviewee will probably never meet again. So the respondent has no compunction to give the right answer, particularly when that answer could lead to embarrassment.

- *Distress purchase.* Filling in questionnaires or answering surveys is a little like buying petrol for one's car. It is a distress purchase: most people would rather be doing something else, particularly if they see that the survey is of little value to them personally. They want shot of the thing, so give answers just to get rid of the questioner.

- *Timing.* The time of the day when one conducts a survey can have a remarkable effect on the results. In the 1992 UK elections, it was widely expected that Labour would defeat John Major's out-going government. The opinion polls got it spectacularly wrong: Major won. One of the reasons quoted was that the polls were conducted between 5pm and 6pm in the evening. The theory was that since Labour could draw greater support from the unemployed (who would be at home) than the employed (who would still be at work), the results were skewed.

These are just a number of factors, and no doubt there are many more reasons which psychologists might give us to explain the disparity between what people say and what they really believe. In controversial projects, all of these factors come heavily into play.

Quantitative market research involves some form of questionnaire where the respondent either answers questions orally or fills in a form. There are numerous ways of undertaking this exercise: some try to pick a representative sample, others do not. Some target who they want responses from, others are just questionnaires left for anyone to fill in. However, they have one common factor: they attempt to mimic a true democratic poll. They are highly dangerous tools, particularly when used by classically trained PR people on a sensitive project.

As the market research professional said at the beginning: What results do you want? This is highly relevant with questionnaires. Who designs it? What order are the questions put in? For example:

- Do you believe that the levels of burglary should be lowered? Yes.
- Do you believe that prison is a good deterrent to burglars? Yes.
- However, prisons are overcrowded and burglars are being released early on parole – sometimes to re-offend immediately. Do you think more prisons are the answer? Yes.
- So you are in favour of the new prison being proposed in your neighbourhood?

This sort of funnelling is, of course, wrong and the example used goes against all the best practice of market research, but it is subtly (much more so than this crude example) and widely used. The results are not only inaccurate – they are highly dangerous. Very few people want a prison near them, even if they are forced to admit it in a survey like this, where they are faced with their own irrationality. The organisation that proceeds on the basis that a majority (according to a flawed survey) said they would like a prison near them will quickly – and painfully – find out the real views.

The next problem is how to ensure that the sample is representative. If the questionnaires are handed out at an exhibition, it is always those who most vociferously oppose who answer. This just embarrasses the promoter of the project, as it now seems there is huge and widespread opposition. If they are posted through front doors, they will – in all likelihood – be totally ignored, except again by those who strongly oppose, with exactly the same effect.

Then, these questionnaires provide great ammunition for those who oppose – in particular, the green groups, who have great pleasure in trawling over each question and interpreting the results in a totally different way from that intended. Naturally, they will also claim that the questionnaire has been rigged and that questions have been funnelled. These accusations are very hard to counter, as in a controversial project, no matter which way one orders the questions, they still look funnelled.

Finally, what use are the results of the questionnaire? What help is it to a firm to know that 89 per cent of people vociferously oppose their project? That was probably known at a much earlier stage.

All in all, these questionnaires are, at best, near to useless and, at worst, highly dangerous.

This is particularly so if these surveys are conducted among politicians.

THE TELEPHONE SURVEY

A company was embarking on a major and highly controversial project. Almost immediately, it was very obvious that there was substantial public and political resistance. After about a year, the company decided to undertake a telephone survey to see if the mood had changed. They hired a market research company to undertake a telephone survey of key politicians.

The survey results showed that – despite a fairly intensive public relations campaign – the mood against the project had hardened substantially. Politicians who had previously expressed some reservations were now set firmly against.

Analysis
If one looks at this exercise from the point of view of the politician, a very different picture emerges.

First, they are rung out of the blue, by someone they don't know and whom they have never met. Naturally, they are immediately on their guard. For all they know this could be a journalist, someone from a rival political party or a green group up to one of its japes.

Therefore, they adopt the first rule of survival in the civil service – cover your back: you can't get in trouble for repeating something that has already been said if it did not cause trouble first time around. So politicians revert to well-tried statements. As they have nothing to lose with this interviewee, they tend to use the statements they know have not caused controversy with their constituents.

Invariably, as most of the people are against the project, they concentrate on the negative statements. In addition, they decide to send a fairly unequivocal message.

THE TELEPHONE SURVEY *(cont'd)*

As they are not sure who the person on the other end of the line is, all the other sides of the arguments – in other words, any positive thoughts they might have on the scheme – are not aired. They also hide these positive statements, as politicians are well used to being quoted out of context and they are well aware of the dangers of the injudicious phrase.

Therefore the results of this survey are difficult not only to validate but also to quantify, as the real views of the politicians have probably remained hidden.

All of this is, in no way, to decry the use of quantitative market research, which has enormous benefit in finding customers' preferences. But customer is the key word: the implication that someone wants to buy. In controversial projects, these methods have very little use. In fact, they can have a negative effect.

Qualitative market research
Realising the limitations of quantitative market research techniques, recent years have seen a move to more qualitative methods – the most popular of which is the focus group. Political parties in particular like these as they give an extra dimension of understanding. However, they too have limitations when dealing with very controversial projects:

- *Overemphasis on the negative.* Almost by definition, a controversial environmental project is one that is meeting very high levels of resistance. Getting a number of people into a room can simply have the effect of confirming what was already known: that the project and its promoters are hated and despised. The one real use of this is to bring along the chief executive of the company or other senior directors to let them observe the discussion from behind a two-way mirror. It often has a calming effect on those testosterone-filled individuals who are demanding action from a hapless public relations department.

- *The moderator.* The success or failure of qualitative market research is hugely dependent on the quality of the moderator – the person who leads the group discussion. By our very nature as human beings, we all have preconceived ideas, perceptions and prejudices. It is very difficult to leave these at the door, even for the most well-trained and well-meaning moderator.

In addition, unless the moderator is particularly good, it can be difficult to stop the group turning into a mob. This is particularly so if alcohol has been used as a tongue loosener.

- *The ego tripper.* Put a dozen people in a room and you are going to get one who wants to shout down everyone else, who believes he or she knows the answer to everything and who wants to dominate the group. Often one can find two of these in the same group which can lead to chaos. Of course, one can filter these out when the group is being formed, but then how representative is it?

The one useful outcome from these exercises is that they often bring forward the beginnings of some ideas of what the group – or individuals within it – might consider are the modifications that are needed in order to make the project less objectionable.

For the most part, focus groups are private, so do not upset the dynamic of the community. They are far more accurate and preferable to mass quantitative methods.

Consensus conferences and citizens' juries

These spring from continental Europe and aim to get opposing views aired in front of members of the public. According to the UK Centre for Economic and Environmental Development (UKCEED), the main aim of a consensus conference 'is to influence the policy-making process by opening up a dialogue between the public, experts and politicians'.

It works by having a forum at which a citizens' panel of about 20 – selected from the general public – questions expert witnesses, weighs the responses it gets, then reaches conclusions which are reported back at a press conference. UKCEED admits that, despite the title, there is no compunction to reach a 'consensus' at the conference: rather the participants 'are encouraged to exploit the extent to which they agree'.

Unlike the hands-on public consultation days (see next section), these make some effort to be representative and this is both their strength and their weakness. The conferences work by first appointing an advisory committee of eight to ten – which is balanced and objective. This is not an easy task and compromises will have to made along the way – especially when you get diametrically opposing views even at this stage. Naturally, a number of highly vocal but unelected green groups usually feature on this group. However, it is rare to find any elected representatives. The democratic system is abandoned at an early stage.

Neither is selecting the witnesses an easy task, but it is not as difficult as one can err on the side of having too many rather than too few. The real problem comes in selecting the citizens' panel. There is a story from the early days of market research which illustrates the problem: 'Be careful with your answer,' says the interviewer, 'it represents the views of three million people.' This is an acceptable risk in market research but it is the selection of the citizens' panel itself that is fraught with danger. According to UKCEED, it is 'carefully selected to reflect a variety of socio-demographic criteria'. However, it admits that: 'The [panel] is too small to be a statistically representative sample of the population... but should reflect as wide a range of views as possible.'

So what sort of person would volunteer to appear on such a panel on the subject, say, of biotechnology or the disposal of radioactive waste? (Selection either involves advertisements in the media or selection by a market research company.) Rightly, the organisers are looking for citizens who 'have not had any significant prior involvement with the conference topic'. In order to participate, citizens must read a comprehensive information pack and attend two preparatory weekends. So who would attend?

Half of the population has an IQ that is below average. Will they offer themselves as concerned citizens? Probably not. Certainly, the organisers may point to the occupation of the participants as evidence of socio-demographic diversity, but this means nothing. (A taxi driver won one of the UK's most arduous TV quizzes, *Mastermind,* in the 1980s.) People who sat at the back of the class all their lives are not suddenly going to come to the front to be made fools of.

It is not so long ago that wide sections of the electorate were disenfranchised for a number of reasons: because they did not own land in the UK, until the 19th century; because they were women, until the 20th century; because they were black, until 25 years ago in parts of the USA. These exercises can introduce a new class system – intelligence or education. Because one is not clever enough to absorb some fairly complex facts, one can be disenfranchised from this exercise. Put simply: you can't vote because you are not smart enough. A frightening prospect for democracy.

Naturally, all of this work needs our old friend the 'independent facilitator' or moderator who 'is responsible for group dynamics, ensuring all panel members have an input, and assisting in writing the final report'. The facilitator should have no influence on the deliberations of the panel or on the content of the report. This is a very tall order indeed.

Hands-on public consultation days

Here, there is an open day or half-day in which members of the public are invited to a meeting room, where they can get involved in hands-on fashion with a project that is about to affect them. Again, the old problem of how to make them representative arises. The hard-line opponents – usually the green groups – tend to boycott them, perhaps mounting a photogenic press call outside the hall. They then claim the exercise is unrepresentative because they have not been involved! The media lap all this up.

Those who turn up usually have their own secret agenda. At a recent event on the development of a new town potentially for 10,000 people, only 60 members of the public turned up – including three vicars. On a representative basis, that would put the number of Christian clergymen in the UK at three million. The vicars were after a new church in the town and – with a substantial number of lay disciples – they made a convincing case for a landmark building (a church with a spire, for example, they gently hinted) to be part of the design. Was this representative? Of course not. These events are not representative at all.

The next problem is how to deal with some of the more imaginative suggestions put forward by members of the public. From the event just mentioned, the more imaginative suggestions included building a new monorail to bringing the existing motorway underground. None of these suggestions is cheap or practical. But how do you explain to the person who has suggested them that these ideas are to be ignored?

Most authorities – be they governments, councils or local communes – have professionals on their staff to deal with the technicalities of a project. The public is – by definition – not professional. They have elected people called politicians to represent them (in fact in many democracies the elected people are called representatives). If they are dissatisfied with the views of the professionals, then they can fire them.

However, although they abhor these events, politicians are almost duty bound to turn up – especially if their own organisation has been in some peripheral way involved in the organisation of the event. However, they do not want to participate. Politicians are nervous creatures and so they come there to observe, definitely not to participate. They are, of course, the representatives of their communities and so are slow to form opinions until they are fairly certain that these opinions reflect the views of these communities.

This brings a new quandary: they do not want to participate, neither do they like to be in the audience, it is not their natural place. They have been elected as leaders and representatives of their communities. They are above them – their place is at the front. By treating them as mere members of the public, they feel – rightly – disenfranchised. This can breed resentment and antagonism.

The problem with these events is that one gets a lop-sided view of a single issue. It is an unrepresentative view that does not reflect the opinions of the population as a whole. While espousing the need for public consultation, politicians know that they will have to live with the consequences and that, in any event, they can do what they want until the next election – never far from the front of the mind in the political animal.

Naturally, the green groups and other minority interests love all these exercises simply because they themselves are so unrepresentative. An organisation which can poll only 5 per cent at an election can have a huge majority at an open day or consensus conference, if they decide to attend. As for the consultation processes, the green groups (now known as non-government organisations, or NGOs) are at the top table, even though they have no democratic remit to represent anyone but themselves and their issues.

Consultation is certainly necessary and it must be public and accessible. However, consultation is always about ideas that are already fairly well formed. The promoter then asks the public what they think. Then it is back to the drawing board to revise the proposals as far as is practical. By encouraging the public to think that they can design the scheme from scratch is bound to generate both resentment and frustration. These feelings are then taken out on the politicians who are roped into a process not of their making.

Consensus conferences and the like are exercises for the middle classes by the middle classes. By their very format, they disenfranchise whole sections of the community. And these sections are entitled to a view – and they want to use it: turn-outs at elections are usually about 75 per cent. Politicians are not stupid, they recognise that in a democracy every vote carries the same weight and, while they may pay lip service to these exercises, they know that they can be safely ignored.

What will work?

In the last chapter, we saw that by approaching people – in an open and honest fashion – one can very quickly get near the truth. This is particularly so if they are asked for their opinions on a one-to-one basis. Maybe it is the sheer simplicity of this approach that makes it unpopular. For a large organisation – particularly those with strong marketing departments – there seems to be a lack of control, a lack of 'guaranteed outcome.'

But it is always fascinating to see how minimal people's demands are: often, for a politician, it is little more than to be allowed to fulfil his or her elected role: to represent the people. Talking to them, meeting them and, most important, listening to them is the way to do this. Giving the democratically elected politicians the information to do their job, allowing them to come to *their* understanding of the project and by allowing them to buy into it by being flexible, is all part of the way forward – the democratic way.

Conclusion

The problem with both questionnaires and the various forms of so-called public consultation is that they are designed to second-guess the democratic system. In effect, they are saying to the people: ignore those people you have elected and come to your own views instead on a particular issue. Taken a step further, it is saying that you cannot trust the politicians, that there are others who know better.

Naturally, politicians tend to react to all of this with a sense of horror and, rightly, resentment. It is brave organisation that undertakes these processes.

Overall, market research is of limited use (probably only the qualitative side) when dealing with very controversial projects. In addition, it should be remembered that – in a modern democracy – what the people think is not of great importance once the election is over. It is what their elected representatives think that is important. Of course, the politicians cannot go against the broad will of their people, but there are times when unpopular decisions have to be taken.

Responsible politicians throughout the ages have bitten the bullet and voted through projects that were meeting with widespread public resistance – from the Eiffel Tower to Brent Spar.

13

Dealing with the Media

Green is a good story and media like the underdog. Journalists often see themselves as consumer champions so empathise with the green groups. But more important, green groups can deliver a good 'shock horror story'. Their real power is the power to accuse and highlight – their focus is entertainment first, information second. Politicians like and hate the media – they speak the same basic language.

Sex, lies and videotape – to inform or to entertain?

People have a low level of trust in the media. According to the 1998 British Social Attitude survey, quoted in the *UK Press Gazette*, only 15 per cent of the population trust the country's journalists to pursue the truth. In addition, people have little or no respect for journalists, rating them just above estate agents.

What, then, is the problem? Why not ignore the media? After all, if no-one believes or trusts the media, why should any organisation care about them? The answer is a fairly simple one and was first formulated by Cohen in 1963 in the book *The Press and Foreign Policy* (Princeton University Press):

> The press may not be successful much of the time in telling people what to think, but it is stunningly successful in telling its readers what to think about.

It is this ability to act as a spotlight that gives the media such power. It is fairly well accepted in most corporate cultures that the person who controls the agenda and the minutes is in a very powerful position. This is

THE MEDIA AND BRENT SPAR

Shell, the co-owner of the redundant oil platform Brent Spar, decided that the best way to get rid of it was to sink it in the North Atlantic. This was after careful analysis – much of it carried out and verified by independent experts. Here it would join thousands and thousands of tonnes of other scrap metal, much of it from warships of the two world wars.

There was nothing radical in any of this. So what made it one of the great environmental cause célèbres of the late 20th century? The answer is the media – in particular, television. TV stations took video footage from Greenpeace and broadcast it to the world. Effectively, it took raw press releases from Greenpeace and, with a little light editing, broadcast them. The agenda was set. And having set the agenda, the minutes soon followed over the next weeks.

The Brent Spar incident – as a media event – could not have happened without media complicity. Complicity is not too strong a word – in many ways, it is too soft. In the words of one BBC executive his organisation 'was led by the nose' by Greenpeace. The media were not only compliant, they were duped. Greenpeace made mistakes – in particular it had to apologise to Shell as some of its 'scientific' testing proved totally erroneous. However, the damage was done and the result was that the Brent Spar was not sunk.

Analysis
Despite Greenpeace getting a little egg on its face – not for the error on its testing, but for deigning to apologise – it was a famous victory for the green groups. And it was made possible by the media.

exactly where the media sit. They can set the agenda and then write the minutes.

So people expect the media to be inaccurate, they do not even expect to read the truth in their newspapers, so why are the media not only read but also heeded in these circumstances?

Entertain them and you can tell them anything, bore them and you can tell them nothing.

So runs the old adage. For the most part, a telephone book is an ideal example of a medium which is pure information: nothing but lists of names, addresses and numbers in small, closely set type. The Yellow Pages is different, here there is advertising which, while seeking to inform – through this advertising – also seeks to entertain and consequently, to influence a buying decision.

In the 19th century, newspapers consisted of pages and pages of type as the technology to reproduce photographs was not readily available. Leaving aside the particular spin of the articles and the prejudices of the authors, this was as near to pure information as one could get.

Slowly, headlines – many banks of them eventually – were brought in. These headlines were designed to stimulate readers' interest – the hook to get them into the article. Eventually, these headlines became bigger and they helped influence the buying decision of the readers as they chose between the various offerings on the newsagent's shelf.

Newspapers were now designed and the design element became as important and, in some cases more important, than the information content. In the words of the Canadian pundit Marshall McLuhan – *the medium had become the message*. Style had overtaken content.

Today, even the most staid of news programmes looks for entertainment value – they have no choice, the battle for readers, listeners and viewers is a fierce one. News, for the most part is intrinsically boring. People say they find politics 'boring', far away wars in little known countries have little impact.

News only becomes interesting when it becomes entertaining. That is the role of the media. Entertainment comes in many forms, but by far the two best components remain those that are well recognised in Hollywood: sex and violence. Brent Spar was violence at its Hollywood best. We all knew no-one would be killed, there was a great big baddie in the shape of Shell and the good guys in the shape of Greenpeace. No wonder the BBC and the rest were led by the noses to transmit it: this was high-grade entertainment.

What is the truth?

However, this drive to entertain can have a frightening effect on the truth. In newspaper offices the talk is not of 'news' or 'facts' but of 'stories'. This is a strong and tacit acceptance that the media have a role to play in 'telling a story'. In fact, in the cynical world of newspapers, there is an adage which says: 'Never let the facts get in the way of a good story.'

In a court of law, witnesses are asked to swear they will tell the 'truth, the whole truth and nothing but the truth.' So what is the difference between the 'truth', the 'whole truth' and 'nothing but the truth'. Why are there three elements? In an adversarial system of justice such as the British one, the prosecution (the state) can intentionally hide pieces of evidence which would be beneficial to the defendant, but detrimental to the prosecution case. Is this 'nothing but the truth'?

By definition, no piece of news can be completely accurate. Editors are, after all, editors. But editing, by its very definition, distorts the truth, even if it is done with the best intention and in an unbiased way. Ironically, the fewer words that a medium has to play with, the more accurate the story is likely to be. So, for example, a 30-minute television news bulletin may contain 15 separate news items and between 2,000 and 3,000 words. This is about one page on a fairly dense broadsheet such as the *New York Times*, but covering only three or four stories.

Therefore, editors have a very difficult job. They have to select the facts, and assemble them in such a way as to present what they believe is as complete a picture as possible which represents the truth.

But there are two factors which can lead to deviation. The first is the need to entertain, and the second is the need to meet the expectations and aspirations of the media's audience. Therefore, a reader of the *News of the World*, a UK Sunday newspaper which specialises in scandals, would be shocked if he were suddenly presented with four pages of carefully argued economic analysis. Similarly, readers of the *New York Times* would not expect to see topless young women disporting themselves on page 3.

THE *SUN* AND LIVERPOOL FOOTBALL CLUB

Liverpool were playing Nottingham Forest at Hillsborough football stadium in Sheffield in 1989. There was a dreadful tragedy where 96 football supporters were crushed to death. Naturally, Britain's most popular newspaper, the *Sun*, covered the story and in a follow-up article suggested that some fans from Liverpool had been drunk and had looted the bodies of the dead.

Not surprisingly, this caused a huge furore in the still grief-stricken city of Liverpool and there was a tremendous local outcry. There were calls for the paper to be withdrawn from sale and boycotted. Almost ten years later in the House of Commons, a local MP, David Watts, said: 'We know that Liverpool fans did not contribute to their own deaths, although the police attempted to blame their behaviour and accused them of being drunk. I believe that Merseyside people will never forget or forgive South Yorkshire police or the *Sun* newspaper. To this day, many newsagents in Liverpool will not take copies of the *Sun*.'

Even now, sales of the *Sun* in Liverpool are still well down on what they were before the report, despite apologies from the newspaper.

In newspaper terms, the looting story was a 'good one'. In terms of news value, it was unpalatable for a substantial number of readers, not just because it was inaccurate, but because it offended the sensibilities of these readers.

Ever since the penny dreadfuls of Victorian times, readers of newspapers have liked to be shocked, in much the same way as people like horror films. However, there is a line, and newspaper editors have to be careful not to transgress it.

On environmental issues, newspapers are on fairly safe ground. Everyone wants to save the planet. So, anyone who causes any detriment to the planet is a fair target. Naturally, of course, newspapers that take up a vast acreage of forest for newsprint and use some nasty chemicals in the printing process are exempt, as are broadcasters who cause visual intrusion with their masts.

The environmental correspondent

Twenty-five years ago few media had an environmental correspondent. Today, there are few which do not have at least one reporter whose job is to cover this issue. When an editor decides to hire someone for this job, what thoughts are going through his or her mind?

It's very simple: circulation numbers (newspapers and magazines) or audience reach (radio and TV). Put simply, it's a numbers game. If the numbers go down, the editor goes out. So, there is huge pressure to get the numbers up. Traditionally, the main way to do this was through improved editorial.[1]

Therefore, stories must be found which will entertain the audience and not offend. So to get back to our question, how will the editor brief the environmental correspondent? Will the brief be:

We have many large corporations and other organisations in our area. I think it would be a good idea if we could show what a splendid and careful job they are doing to protect the environment. Indeed, I believe some have won awards for this work. For a start we could concentrate on those companies who are accredited with the environmental standard ISO 14001.

This cannot happen. It is boring. It's not entertaining. The brief is much more likely to go along the following lines:

The environment is a huge issue for our readers/audience. They are concerned about it and we need to reflect that concern. The environmental groups seem to be fairly good at finding out the dirt on local firms. Get fairly close to the open-sandled lentil eaters [editors tend not to mince their words] and bring in some cracking tales.

Now many would think the key skill of a reporter is a facility with English, an ability to encapsulate difficult facts precisely into simple language. But overriding this is the quality of the reporter's contacts: who he or she knows. So our reporter, having been appointed, immediately makes a bee-line for the green groups. In fact, they probably meet half-way. The green groups – excelling as they do at media relations – have already heard about the new appointment and – like star-crossed lovers – they dash headlong into each other's arms.

There now forms a useful symbiotic relationship. The green group provides the environmental correspondent with a steady supply of shock-horror stories, which in turn keeps the editor happy, as they both entertain and appease the audience.

But surely there must be balance. Of course, it is called the balancing comment. When the reporter has written the shock-horror story, the organisation is then approached for a comment 'to balance out the piece'. Even if the company manages to say something strong and sensible, or even manages totally to refute the story as a tissue of lies, this will appear at the very bottom of the story.

Of course, reporters and editors are aware that there is a huge decay curve in how newspaper stories, in particular, are read. Nearly everyone reads the headlines, but by the time they get to the balancing comment, only a tiny proportion of the readers remain. The headline itself is 90 per cent of the impact, and if the sub-editor has any qualms about one, such as 'Local Firm will Wipe Out Last of the Newts', it is put into quotation marks – after all, the green group did say it.

Influencing the media

Given all of this, media relations are not surprisingly very difficult for large organisations. And it seems very simple for the green groups. Like life, it is not fair, or is it? Perhaps these groups are the real experts at public relations – hence their levels of success.

They are incorporating the five factors of good media relations in environmental issues:

- Independence
- Non-profit making
- Underdogs

■ Freedom to express themselves
■ Absolute in demands.

Compared to most large organisations, the green groups have a number of very substantial advantages in all five factors.

■ *Independence.* The green groups are seen as independent 'watch-dogs' – in fact, they are often referred to as such by the media. The fact that they are pressure groups with their own powerful agendas is not obvious to the media, or else they choose to ignore it.

■ *Non-profit making.* In the UK, most of the green groups are registered charities. As well as giving them very substantial tax breaks, this status also gives an aura of altruism.

■ *Underdogs – The David syndrome.* Everyone loves the underdog. Compared to large corporations, the green groups are very good at presenting themselves as Davids to Goliaths. The fact that an organisa-tion like Greenpeace has a very respectable turnover of £100 million and hundreds of employees is overlooked. The green groups play up to this image with tales of frugality: in fact, salaries in most of these groups – particularly Greenpeace – are very good indeed.

■ *Speculation.* One of the most powerful tools in the armoury of the green groups are words like 'could', 'might', 'it is feared', and so on. Whereas most organisations are constrained from speculating, this does not apply to the green groups. And, of course, they are fully entitled to speculate and often this – if taken to its extreme – could have terrible consequences. Naturally, this makes for very good stories for the media.

In the Brent Spar incident, Greenpeace initially accused Shell of wanting to dump the platform in the North Sea. In fact, it was the North Atlantic – a totally different stretch of water. A Greenpeace spokesperson discounted this as being immaterial – it's the principle that counts. This, of course, is the same organisation that demands meticulous accuracy from all of those it attacks.

■ *The law of the absolute.* This demands that any action can never cause any detriment to anyone, anywhere or at any time. Of course, this is an impossible condition to meet. All actions cause some detriment. What is important is that this be contained and that remedial measures are put in place to mitigate and compensate for the detriment. For journalists, the law of the absolute is very powerful. To the question: 'So, can you guarantee that this initiative you are about to undertake will cause no damage whatsoever...?', the answer 'yes' is, in all probability, untrue. So, for example, how safe is the word 'safe'? Is the pencil I am holding in my hand safe if I decide to stick it in someone's eye? But the full answer will not fit into a 15-second sound bite. A victory for the green groups who can rightly call for all pencils to be banned on the grounds that they are unsafe.

How journalists mirror the green groups

These characteristics make the green groups very powerful in media terms. It is always dangerous to stereotype, but these characteristics could equally be applied to many reporters:

- *Independence*. Naturally, reporters see themselves as independent. Many would go to prison rather than compromise their code of ethics – and have done since the earliest days of *The Times of London* when its editor John Walter went to prison rather than reveal his sources of information, so founding a tradition which lasts to this day.

- *Not profit-making*. Rupert Murdoch may be one of the richest men in the world, but it is the media moguls who make the money. Many journalists decry the status of the industry which they now see as being run by 'money men' rather than by journalists and editors. It's probably just as well the money men are running the media, otherwise there might be no media.

   In addition, journalists are notoriously badly paid. A newly qualified reporter (probably with a primary degree) joining a provincial newspaper in the UK earns about £10,000 per annum. This compares with up to £20,000 for graduate trainees joining banks and legal practices.

- *The David syndrome*. Many journalists are attracted to the profession as they are drawn to the investigative element. The media are very powerful and they can use this force to protect the 'little guys'. In addition, there is the watchdog role on large organisations, which they hope to fulfil.

- *Speculation*. Newspapers are full of it – it's meat and drink. In the run-up to elections, speculation runs rife and becomes the mainstay of the papers. As any reader of an astrology column will tell, speculation is also fun, which gives it a high entertainment value, vital to gain audience share.

- *The law of the absolute.* 'People are simple folk and they are busy – the role of the journalist is to sift the facts and tell them what's right and wrong.' The media have to make judgements on what is right and what is wrong. Too often there is only black and white.

Does this mean that the media and journalists are prejudiced? Of course, we all harbour prejudices, whether we like to admit them or not. This is natural and normal. And, of course, with huge levels of green consciousness and conscience displayed by the media's audience, it is not surprising that this is reflected in what is produced.

Dealing with the media

So what can a large organisation do? The response of most is based on classical public relations. However, the problem with classical PR is that it is based on consumerism. Here, the customer is willing to buy (or at least is wanting to consider buying) the product. In issues communications, the opposite is true. There is antagonism towards the company.

Compare, for example, buying a new car and having an incinerator in your village. In the first case, you are happy to read about the model you wish to buy: in fact, the more glowing the press reports, the more reassured you are about your buying decision. In the case of the incinerator, you want to believe everything that is bad. And you definitely will not believe anything the promoting organisation wishes to tell you about. 'They would say that, wouldn't they?'

The major media tactics used by companies are numerous.

Press releases

In dealing with environmental issues, press releases issued by a company have a number of problems:

- *Lack of continuity.* For any communications to be effective, they need to be intensive. For example, TV advertisements are repeated many times in order to have the desired effect. The problem for large companies is that – after the first press release – they run out of things to say. In addition, by its very definition news is new. Newspaper editors are not in the business of re-running stories.

- *Journalistic cynicism.* In addition, these releases are viewed cynically by journalists. As well as 'they would say that, wouldn't they?', there is a lingering impression that an organisation is only releasing the good news and suppressing the bad.

▪ *Previous record.* Often, press releases talk of improvements to the company's facility. A new piece of kit will lead to major environmental benefits. These 'I have stopped beating my wife' releases fail for exactly that reason: why did you beat her in the first place?

▪ *Door opening.* Never open a door that you cannot shut. A press release is a public document and puts the company in the spotlight. Is everything else in order or will the release just cause a number of other awkward questions to be asked? For example, you have fixed this plant, but how about the others, which are still filthy?

▪ *The legal department.* A press release is effectively a statement of company policy. Therefore, it will have to be vetted by a number of people, not least the legal department. (If your legal department is not vetting your press releases – well, good luck – you now have a real problem.) These cautious folk can very quickly emasculate a strong press release into nothing, as the following fictitious example shows.

PROTECTING THE ENVIRONMENT

A large investment in research and development (R&D) and a commitment to a newly developed filtration process, mean that the effluent coming out of the SupaClean Inc. chemical manufacturing plant at Troutsville is now of higher quality than ever.

SupaClean Inc. has an ongoing R&D programme called 'Clean & Clear', whose primary objective is to produce water that is cleaner and clearer. Launched in 1994, the team of ten scientists have been forging the way in water treatment processes within the chemical manufacturing industry.

Director of the Clean & Clear programme, Dr Thomas Michel, said, 'SupaClean's water filtration process is backed by cutting-edge technology and the company's keen philosophy of environmental responsibility. SupaClean has always sought to achieve the highest standards in all aspects of the business, not merely on the products we manufacture.

'I am very proud of our achievements. Not many chemical manufacturers can say that their water is as clean as ours.'

PROTECTING THE ENVIRONMENT *(cont'd)*

SupaClean has a firm commitment to the environment and a keen interest in the River Fleuve. Coupled with such projects as the Fleuve Mallard Duck nesting programme, a SupaClean initiative launched in 1996, SupaClean is shaping the face of tomorrow's chemical industry.

Obviously, this is pure flannel and totally content free, which makes the lawyers happy. Press releases like this – and there are a lot of them – will change neither a company's position nor journalists' perception of it. In fact, they do damage as editors can quickly see drivel as such.

The initial version of the release made a claim that the quality of the effluent was now higher than the quality of river water – a good story until the lawyers got hold of it.

Press releases tend to suffer from all the problems of marketing-led communications outlined in the last chapter. They are certainly attractive to organisations because of the ability to resource them and, when successful, they are a very cost-effective mechanism. There are a number of problems with press releases in contentious issues.

The intent of the release
The first question to be asked in issues management is: why do we want to send out a press release? Often, sending out a press release is autonomic – it's what we always do. This can be reinforced if the public relations department has a number of ex-journalists: we all tend to gravitate to that which we know best. Of course, if it is a major change of policy or some such, then a press release is appropriate.

The same impact may be achieved by a few letters to key individuals, or even by a telephone conversation.

THE PRICE RISE

A major utility issues a press release saying that it is going to have a price rise, but couches the press release in terms of its huge investment programme which will bring benefits to customers.

THE PRICE RISE *(cont'd)*

Investment in water quality up by 7 per cent

Valley Water Plc today announced that it was to increase its
investment programme by 7 per cent in the next financial year.
This will lead to a number of improvements in water quality
and security of supply. [There then follow five more para-
graphs outlining the investment programme.] The company
also announced today that its prices would only rise by 5 per
cent for the next year, well below the level of investment.

What does the newspaper editor do? Get the views of the local old age
pensioners on fixed incomes and ask how they will be affected. There is
not a mention of the investment programme. In effect, he goes looking for
a third party. This is the headline which appeared:

Shock as water bills spurt 7%

They're a shower of drips, says pensioner

If you have bad news to announce to the media, the best way to do it
is through route one – the direct, open and honest way. Put the news up
front. In addition, do not drip-feed bad news. The company which
announces that it had a small leak of effluent gets some bad headlines on
the day. However, if that leak – after investigations by the regulatory
authorities – turns out to be 40,000 gallons, then it is another bad story –
how the company tried to cover up the original 'small' leak.

The impact of the release
When one is dealing with contentious issues, the mere fact of actually
sending out a press release is a significant event in its own right. But the
impact of the press release as it lands on the journalist's desk is difficult to
gauge.

The journalist may decide on a number of courses of action:

1. Put it in the bin – often the least dangerous from the organisation's
   point of view.

2. Check in the cuttings library to see what has happened on this issue previously. In this case, the organisation must be aware and be ready to defend everything that has happened in the past.

3. Call the opposition to get their views. The press release can then be turned on its head, with the protest or green group getting their message across instead of the organisation that issued the press release.

The use of the release

However, press releases do not have the same level of control as that offered by advertising. One has to allow another individual – this time a journalist – to alter the content before it can be used.

There is one sure fact about the press release: it will seldom be used verbatim. (Of course, certain media will often take advertorial and use the press release exactly, but they usually demand advertising support – which, in effect, makes it advertising by any other name. Other lazy media will use it verbatim, but by definition, this type of outlet has no clout and is useless.) And, as noted earlier, if the journalist is any good he or she will need balancing comment, but in this case it is to balance your arguments and to counter them.

A useful exercise is to role play the journalist in one of the media to which you would like to send the press release, and then judge the likely reactions – what he or she will do when they get it. If you do not know the answer to this, you are effectively walking in the dark carrying in your hand a grenade with the pin pulled out.

Attempt to write the story as they might write it: we have noted that many organisations have ex-journalists in their PR department, so this is a fairly simple exercise. However, it may not be a very pleasant one. When the finished article is passed around senior management, it often tempers their enthusiasm for using the press as a mechanism of influence.

Now decide if you really need to send out this press release.

Press conferences

As with all public meetings (dealt with in detail in Chapter 13), these are best avoided. In effect, they are a form of intellectual foxhunting. The fox is the company, which decides to break cover, the beaters are the green groups and the hounds are the journalists.

A curious dynamic arises in press conferences. First, the journalists often try to out-nasty each other, each thinking of tougher and tougher

questions to put to the respondents. Conversely, the cleverer journalists
hold back their good questions so that they are not pilfered by the others,
and ask them privately at the end.

Of course, there are times – for example, in the middle of a major
crisis – when a press conference is a good way of disseminating a
substantial amount of information in an open and fair way. But they have
only limited use in the world of issues management.

Given that two of the major tools – press releases and press conferences – do not work well, what is left? There are a number of techniques
that are highly effective in dealing with the media, which allow a company
to get across its point in a fair and accurate way. All of these techniques
are widely used by the green groups.

One-to-one meetings

These are a vast improvement, but are not used often enough. In a face-to-
face meeting, one can get to know journalists on a personal as well as
professional level. Naturally, journalists are slightly cynical when first
approached. Therefore, it is important to have a story – or at least a
suggestion of a story – to bring to the meeting. Rather like the angel of
death in Denis Wheatley's horror stories (who cannot return to hell
without a human soul), or the kukri – the Gurkha knife which, once
unsheathed, must taste blood being being replaced in its sheath, the journalist must have a story. The company need not write this story – particularly not in the press release format – in advance of the meeting. This more
informal approach allows the journalist to come to the story rather than
have it thrust upon him or her. In this forum, a press release can be seen
as threatening. In addition, if the meeting occurs over lunch, and the press
officer is buying, there is a hint of bribery.

Initially, these meetings are best undertaken by a company press
officer – who will often be a former journalist. If this works well, other
initiatives can be undertaken with the same journalist.

The chief executive

Whereas chief executives have absolutely no place at public meetings (as
we will see in the next chapter), they can have a most useful role in media
relations. In fact, there is little doubt that by far the best PR person in
every company is the chief executive. This is nothing to do with commu-

nication skills, but everything to do with the fact that journalists like to get as near the top as possible to give greater credibility to their stories.

Therefore, one-to-one briefings with known journalists and the chief executive are very fruitful. Ideally, these should be undertaken *without* the presence of a 'minder' in the form of a press officer. Brief the CEO well and then trust him or her. After all, when something has been said, it cannot be unsaid, so the minder has no real role.

Obviously, other members of senior management can also undertake this role, but they are never as powerful as the CEO.

The power of third party advocates with the media

Finding and mobilising third party advocates (TPAs) is dealt with in detail in Part III, but they have a key role in dealing with the media. Too often, they are ignored by companies, for a number of reasons:

- *Reliability*. Large organisations are afraid that the TPA will not say exactly what is required. Of course they won't, but that is what makes them so powerful. Journalists do not want to interview puppets.

- *Control*. Companies like to control all of their statements. However, TPAs are not making company policy in their statements. They are free agents.

- *Availability*. Often, an organisation does not know who its TPAs might be and none is available.

  However, well-placed, informed and articulate TPAs can have a powerful role. They can certainly defend and promote the company strongly, by keying in on the five factors outlined earlier.

- *Independence*. TPAs are, by definition, independent. And they must be kept that way. It is particularly damaging to try to coach them or to get them to be even more favourable. Ironically, a hint of cynicism or antagonism from the TPA makes their statement all the more powerful. So, the following is strong from a TPA:

No, I must disagree – this company has taken every possible precaution to mitigate the damage from its facility. I believe they have now solved the minor problem they had and that all will be well.

However, the following is much stronger:

As you know in the past, I have been critical of the performance of this company. However, I now believe they are making an honest effort to get things right. It is early days still and we should wait and see. But to attack them now just when they are getting their act together is not helpful and one must doubt the motives of those doing so.

The second statement is far more powerful. It is more cautious and less sycophantic – but then that is exactly what makes a good TPA.

TPAs also have many of the characteristics of the green groups and, as noted earlier, there is empathy between these and the media. TPAs are generally not helping a project from a profit motive; often, their involvement is altruistic, although, of course, they may have their own win–win projects. They can speculate openly and even inaccurately and the law of the absolute does not bind them. So, the question: 'Do you think this plant is absolutely safe', can be answered 'yes' without being stuck with caveats.

Rather than the organisation trying to manage its own media relations, they are much more powerful if the TPAs take a hand. This is a good example.

THE SCHOOL AND THE HOUSES

In the overcrowded, developed world, new housing developments are strongly resisted – the NIMBY syndrome. Of course, NIMBYism nearly always dresses itself up in rational clothes – there is too much traffic, the schools and hospitals are over-stretched, and so on. But, new schools and hospitals are seen as good things and their expansion and improvement is a great motherhood cause. However, their expansion can also be resisted if new houses come in their wake. (The irrationality of this argument is mostly lost on the NIMBY brigade: after all, if schools expand, then they can have more pupils, which means more houses.)

So when St Albion's School decided it needed funds to expand, it found that the only way it could raise these funds was to sell land for housing development. The strategy adopted by the school and the developer was fairly simple and obvious: lead with the benefits of the school's expansion. In addition, as the project was mooted in 1999, link it into the excitement that was surrounding the millennium. For this, the school (not the developer) produced a press release.

THE SCHOOL AND THE HOUSES *(cont'd)*

£5 MILLION TO LAUNCH ST ALBION'S INTO THE NEW MILLENNIUM

St Albion's is planning a £5 million investment in much-needed and far-reaching improvements, which will give the school state-of-the-art facilities in the new millennium.

St Albion's headmaster, Geoff Hughes, said: 'We believe this investment will give our pupils some of the best and most modern facilities in the county. This is vital if our pupils are to continue to get not only a good education, but also to have the facilities to become fully rounded individuals in their own right.'

This is what the millennium project will mean for St Albion's:

1. A new state-of-the-art computer unit.
2. A new gymnasium – fully equipped.
3. The end of temporary huts for teaching to be replaced by new classrooms.
4. New sports facilities including an all-weather sports field.

This project will mean that some of the older Victorian buildings will be replaced by ones that are more suited to the needs of a modern school. These will be cheaper and easier to maintain so enabling us to put even more money into education rather than maintenance.

In order to achieve this ambitious and necessary programme, the school will sell some redundant land for the construction of about 40 new houses.

Finally, the new sports facilities would also be open to the wider community, so providing a much-needed and important resource in the area.

The plans are subject to the granting of planning permission from Middleshire District Council and this week an application was submitted to them.

This release has many similarities to the press release on the water price increase. What is considered to be the bad news is buried in the release. However, there is a huge difference – now it is a third party which is issuing the news and it is perfectly legitimate for them to lead with the most important aspect of the project.

The key message
The press release is very useful for print media as they can take direct quotes from it. However, for broadcast media, it is also useful to have a key sound bite prepared. For example, in this last example:

> This is a planning application by the school to improve St Albion's science, arts and recreation facilities for the new millennium. In difficult circumstances, teachers and pupils are getting good results, but with new classrooms the real winners will be local children.

The lifebelt statement
This key message is also the lifebelt statement, which interviewees can use if they get into trouble on the key benefits or defences (if bad news) which are contained in the release. Politicians are masters of this. Their rule is: Always answer the question you had hoped you might be asked.

Questions and answers
A common ancillary to the press release is the question and answer sheet. This is a very useful exercise, which looks at all the difficult questions which might arise from the issuance of the press release.

The Qs and As attempt to cover only potentially contentious issues. The questions are deliberately framed in an aggressive way – such as one might get at a raucous public meeting. They do not cover basic facts that can be gleaned from published information. They should not run to more than two pages, otherwise they would not be properly assimilated or used.

The Qs and As should form a consistent 'hymn sheet' from which there is no deviation. Answers should be formulated in such a way as to make the answers specific, but also broad enough to be used as statements for other questions.

There are some fairly simple rules surrounding these Qs and As.

1. They should not state the obvious facts – they should only deal with that which is contentious.

2. They should not be more than two pages of A4 – if they are running to more, then you should reconsider whether you actually really want to send out this release at this time. If it's raising more questions than it is answering, then it may be fundamentally flawed.

3. It should not contain any 'landmines'. In other words, there should be no facts buried within it which are not evident from the press release. There is no room for economy with the truth in press releases.

These are some basic guidelines. This is not a book on media relations, and for those with an interest in this area, there are some excellent works available, such as Annie Gurton's *Press Here*, Jossey-Bass, 1998.

Evaluation

There is now a massive growth industry, called media evaluation. This is as old as newspapers: people have been counting column inches for centuries. However, given that people do not have much respect for newspapers (or journalists), how valid is this exercise? If people are sceptical about what they read, then they may not believe it. And if they don't believe it, how valid is the media evaluation exercise?

A guide entitled 'How to get real value from public relations', published in 1997 by the International Committee of Public Relations Consultancies Associations (ICO), says that 'publicity in print and broadcast media remains the biggest single "product" of public relations'. However, publicity alone – even if it is positive (unlikely in issues management) – does not mean a campaign has been successful unless publicity in itself was the sole objective. And this is a total waste of time and money.

According to a survey referred to elsewhere in this pamphlet, those working in the sphere of public relations credit themselves with a good deal of influence in the media. This survey revealed that PR people believed that 40 per cent of media coverage is PR inspired. Interestingly, the journalists estimated this figure at a significantly lower level of 25 per cent – more proof of the dangers of market research.

Too often long-running campaigns lose focus and evaluate immeasurables such as raised awareness, a shift in attitudes, positive media coverage or perceived improvements in reputation. The measurement of these is open to an individual's interpretation. Many PR campaigns do not set specific tangible goals, and so their effectiveness, or ineffectiveness, is never fully understood.

There is a preoccupation with collecting evidence (media evaluation), rather than looking for real proof (did we succeed in what we set out to do?). The emphasis is on measuring actions rather than checking on the result: Did we succeed or fail?

With difficult environmental issues, life is simpler. For the most part, the system of evaluation is binary – there can only be either success or failure. This is a very harsh method and is the only one that works. Ideally, the objective should be simple to state and should have a number (be it a time reference, a cost or whatever).

Here are some examples of good objectives.

- We want to build an incinerator by April 2002.
- We want to increase the number of people using buses by 50 per cent in two years.
- We want the local council to approve plans for the chemical recycling factory by the end of the year.

These sorts of objectives are common in areas such as performance-related pay awards, for example.

From start to finish the campaign must yield tangible results. These results can only be measured by clear facts independent from individual interpretation. For example, how many shoppers have applied for a store card, instead of how many shoppers were offered a store card, or how many shoppers appeared to be aware of the store card? Results should be quantifiable. However, PR is about people and, as sociologists have discovered, measuring and assessing human behaviour in a quantifiable way is inherently problematic. To measure emotions, beliefs and other human factors successfully is difficult, especially as it is a human that is doing the measuring. People are always looking to give the right answer, as opposed to their own real answer.

However, in many cases public relations still harks back to the more aspirational style of objectives. In *Public Relations Research and Evaluation Toolkit* (1999), researched and written by Michael Fairchild and sponsored by the Institute of Public Relations (IPR) and the Public Relations Consultants Association (PRCA), there are eight case studies of successful public relations campaigns.

The following examples show contrasting approaches:

- *Heart disease campaign.* The objective was to heighten the awareness of the risk of coronary heart disease (CHD) – especially among younger people. The campaign was claimed as a success because there was a substantial increase in the number of people who said – in an opinion poll – that they were more aware that CHD could affect them and that the majority had therefore planned life-style changes. Obviously, the real results of this campaign cannot be known for many years – until this current generation begins to die – but one should be very careful about what people tell opinion pollsters. (Remember the garbologists in Chapter 11?)

- *Diamond White cider.* The objective here was to raise the street cred of this youth-oriented brand and to reverse a decline in sales. Both objectives were met – in particular the latter, which was clearly seen in a 13 per cent increase in sales.

These two examples show the diversity of approaches to measurement. The first campaign cannot produce tangible results, whereas the second can. Of course, if you embark on a major media campaign, you are bound to get a change of attitude, or at least people will claim that they have changed a behaviour, but this a tricky area involving market research, which is itself open to question. And the real result will take years to come in: How many fewer heart attacks were there? However, there is no arguing with a 13 per cent increase in sales.

That is not to say that projects should not have fixed deliverables guiding progress and enabling accurate assessment of results. By breaking projects into phases, each with measurable results, the success of the programme can be monitored throughout. Objectives must not only be agreed but also followed up at the appropriate stage of the project.

In a local community project the objectives could be:

1. Complete a diagnostic by April 1.
2. Meet the parish council and the three key local councillors by May 14.
3. Have all modifications agreed with the community by September 1.
4. Get approval for the project by year-end.

This, however, is not proof that the project is on track. These are simple management tools to ensure that certain actions are taken by certain deadlines to maximise the chances of success. A campaign may appear to be running smoothly, but the end-result may prove an unexpected one. For example, the housing development mentioned in Chapter 10: here, the developers were confident, because in terms of traditional PR evaluation the campaign was a success. A site visit had been carried out with positive feedback and the media coverage was equally positive. The development had the support of the local mayor, the officers and the two main political parties. The members, however, rejected the officers' recommendations and the scheme went down.

This example highlights the danger of not evaluating through measuring actions. The campaign could be heralded a success at every stage, and yet it was, ultimately, a failure. During this time a good deal of expensive and ineffective PR will have been carried out – without a successful result.

So, for today's computer-based, seemingly sophisticated media evaluation programmes, it is impossible to know their real impacts in issues-related projects. We do not know what levels of credence people have in individual journalists or news media. People may be reading or listening to something and only partially believing it. There are whole sections of newspapers which are never read – they go straight in the bin yet media evaluation will use multiples of total readership so will come up with an impact.

Certainly, evaluation has a role in providing evidence, but the only real proof is in the end-result of the project. Did it succeed or fail? – the binary approach.

Conclusion

As in all projects in a modern, open democracy, the media have a crucial and important role. However, the organisation that believes it can influence public opinion through a medium which is driven by a need to entertain as well as inform is suffering under a dangerous illusion. The media must be dealt with and the best people to deal with them are third party advocates.

Note

1. Although as Rupert Murdoch has shown with *The Times* newspaper, a far more effective way is to lower the price. This newspaper, which languished with a circulation of 500,000 for years and lost millions, suddenly gained a circulation of 800,000 thanks to massive price cuts. The editorial changed, but few independent commentators would suggest it got that much better.

14 Managing Public Meetings

With the baiting of bears and badgers being now illegal, when miscreants are no longer put in stocks so that the populace can throw rotten fruit at them and the end of feeding Christians to lions, there is a vacuum. However, the nature of mankind does not change so dramatically in a few short centuries, and this need to hunt and mock is still alive and well. Certainly, it is more civilised, but today the public meeting on a contentious project easily fills the void left by the badgers, the bears and the Romans. Of course, that is not to say that all those who attend public meetings do so out of a sense of sadistic voyeurism, but there is an element of excitement, the thrill of the chase, which is naturally attractive to part of the human psyche.

Who attends public meetings?

There is an old joke, that the only problem with public meetings is the public. This is only half true – the public is never the issue, the problem is that the real public never turns up to a public meeting. For a start, public meetings on a contentious issue are usually very sparsely attended. Certainly, a group of 200 angry residents can look daunting, but this must be considered in the context of the total population affected – often numbered in tens of thousands. For many meetings, the number barely climbs into double figures. So this is the first problem with these events – they are not representative, and if they are not representative, they are not democratic. Therefore, they have little value.

The second problem is that meetings can be quickly hijacked, as can be seen by this case.

THE ROYAL SOCIETY REPORT

The UK radioactive waste disposal agency, Nirex, had embarked on a huge scientific research programme to try to find a way to dispose of radioactive waste. Much of this research was on complex ecological issues. Because the issues were so complex, the company gave its results to a very eminent UK body of scientists, the Royal Society, to review and to comment on them.

In broad terms, the Royal Society praised the work, but naturally there were areas it questioned and where it asked for more research. It decided to hold a press conference to announce its results.

Naturally, the green groups – in the shape of Friends of the Earth and Greenpeace – turned up and proceeded to ask the first four or five questions. This was a beautiful piece of agenda setting and predictably, they focused on those parts of the report which were least favourable to Nirex. Such was the frustration of the journalists present that one of them asked for the pressure groups to shut up and let the journalists ask some questions. And this was a press conference.

All public meetings can be subject to this form of hijacking.

The next problem is that the facts are early casualties at a public meeting. Emotion quickly takes over, and what was meant to be an orderly meeting turns into a shouting match with a mob. Emotions rise, and questions like 'Are you prepared to see children impaled on your fence?', or 'Who will stand trial for corporate manslaughter when this scheme goes ahead?' take over from the rational arguments.

Many organisations – in the mistaken belief that rational arguments will prevail – actually set up public meetings. This is the ultimate example of foxes voting for the retention of hunting.

However, there are times when the public meeting becomes inevitable: it has to be held. This may be because it is demanded by a politician or because the consultation mechanism demands it. In fact, most politicians privately hate the thought of public meetings, but see that they must be done in order to have been seen to have completed a full consultation process.

In general, public meetings can be divided into three types:

- *Presentations* – where the organisation makes a presentation of its proposals

- *Exhibitions* – which are held over a number of days and people can wander in and out
- *Liaison groups*. In effect, these are a series of on-going public meetings.

Presentations

At its simplest, this involves representatives of a promoting organisation presenting its proposals to a group of people. Often, the company is the only one to present and there is no independent chairman. This is a recipe for chaos.

Even worse is when two opposing sides put forward their point of view. For example, a company proposing a controversial project and a green group. This best way to describe this is a hunt with a three-legged fox – the company has no chance: the green groups are seen as wanting to protect the environment (so what is the company doing?). The green group is small and non-profit making (and the company?) and the hall is packed with green supporters (the company is too 'genteel' to seek supporters.) In addition, this bypasses the politicians – who were elected – in favour of the green groups who were not. So how do they feel about that?

For these meetings, the opponents are usually well organised with lots of difficult questions. If there are any neutral members of the public, they are immediately presented with a list of horrors that the promoter hopes to foist on them. If there are any supporters, they are quickly intimidated by the strength of the opponents and if they speak out, they are brave indeed.

Despite the obvious tension, these are fairly civilised affairs, as befits a modern society. Often, there will be a round of applause at the end, which may lead the organisation to assume that this presentation has gone down particularly well. No, this is the audience applauding itself for its bravery. Often, a drink is bought for the promoters at the end. This is not friendliness, this is guilt: despite the thrill of the chase, we still do not like to be nasty to our fellow humans.

Rules of engagement
Many companies rush headlong into public meetings, accepting all the conditions which are asked by those organising them. Even if the organiser is neutral (a local council, for example), a company can still gain much by trying to ensure that the playing field is as level as possible. Here are some of the points which can be negotiated:

THE CHAIRMAN

This is an absolutely crucial role. Paradoxically, even a biased chairman is more useful than no chairman at all. If the promoter is in direct conflict with the audience, then it is bare-knuckle fighting without a referee – a street brawl. If the organisation attempts to chair the meeting itself, it will be accused of trying to stifle debate every time it tries to bring order to the meeting or to stop a repetitious speaker.

Ideally, the chairman should be as neutral as possible: local politicians are ideal, if they have not taken sides and are fairly senior. However, few politicians like to get between the lion and his dinner, so they tend to decline these invitations politely – often on the pretext that they have better things to do, which is absolutely true.

However, a chairman is needed and must be insisted upon by the organisation. Otherwise, one should not agree to a meeting – it is a perfectly legitimate excuse to say that one is not willing to have a meeting until a chairman is found.

NOTICE

Once a public meeting has been agreed, it becomes the property of the organisation that is promoting the project. This is so, even if the meeting is being promoted by someone else. In effect, it is your trial, so you should have a real interest in making sure it goes well. Key to this is the amount of notice given for the meeting. If the meeting is called at very short notice, then one will be accused of trying to exclude people.

Most people associate the democratic process with free and fair elections. But there is much more to it than that. All democracies which do not have fixed times for elections insist that a proper period of notice is given. Even snap elections need four to six weeks' notice. There are good reasons for this, such as: candidates should be given time to prepare and organise themselves, and the issues can be debated to give voters a chance to hear as many sides of the argument as they want. The same applies to a public meeting: a good period of notice should be given – at least two to three weeks.

ADVERTISING THE MEETING

Advertise the meeting as widely as possible and let the opponents take a hand in this. Give them leaflets or posters. This may seem foolish, but the fairer the meeting is seen to be, and the more the promoter is seen to try to make it fair, the better the outcome. Given that one is not going to win on the night, the best that can be done is to ensure that one gets some credit for having played fair.

THE UNTIMELY MEETING

A company was promoting a large new industrial area next to an existing housing estate. The land was already zoned for industry which had caused some furore, so it was decided to hold a public meeting.

Like most organisations, this company had normal working hours. So it was not unnatural that they sought to hold the meeting as near to these hours as possible. However, they realised that others also worked and would need to travel, so they picked what they thought was a reasonable time of 6.00pm.

This caused an outcry and rightly so. Here were some of the arguments that were made:

- Traffic is terrible in this area (and, incidentally, your development will make it worse), so it is impossible for people to be at the meeting at 6.00pm.
- Some people have young children and it is difficult to get baby sitters at such a time.
- How long will this meeting go on for? Ideally, most people would like to have their evening meal before attending. Public meetings are never short, so this is a very valid point.

Analysis
The meeting went ahead, but in a particularly foul and bitter atmosphere. The local paper reported briefly on the meeting, but widely on the timing and how this was an attempt to 'gag the local people'.

TIMING

The meeting should be held to ensure that the maximum number of people have the opportunity to attend.

WHO SHOULD SPEAK AT THE MEETING?

Having found a neutral chairman (or as near neutral as possible), careful thought must be given to who else should attend. The following are some candidates:

INDEPENDENTS

Ideal candidates include any type of independent regulator or government official. This includes anyone who has an official role: planning officers from local authorities, officers from the Environment Agency, health and safety inspectors and the like. For the most part, these are seen as neutral. In a controversial project, they bring a number of other attributes:

▪ *Rationality* – which cannot be brought by the promoter of a scheme. The promoters are emotionally involved (they are in the arena – they are engaged in the combat; they have real benefit to gain – which is balanced by a major detriment to the community; they often have financial gain). Therefore, the promoters' rational arguments are shouted down. However, an independent figure can make the same arguments and be listened to, even if reluctantly. It is not even necessary for the regulatory figures to agree fully with the scheme – all that is needed is that the more highly charged accusations against the company are defused.

▪ *Independence*. They have no financial benefit from any scheme, their views are truly independent.

▪ *Their careers*. People accept that as soon as independent regulators are not independent, they are fired. So this person has a different vested interest from the developer – it is a vested interest in maintaining his career. This is easily understood.

THE MAJOR NEW TOWN

In overcrowded parts of the world, where traffic is a major problem, there is strong resistance to further housing developments. However, more houses are needed due to increased population, people living longer and the rising divorce rate leading to more single-occupancy homes.

Central government accepts this and so gets experts to advise on numbers. These numbers are then allocated to local regions and finally to local communities. In one area, 7,000 new houses were proposed next to an existing town. This was not popular and so a public meeting was held. The plan was rejected.

Among the first to speak at the public meeting was an official from the local council, who explained the rationale and logic behind the numbers. He also explained the efforts the council had made to try to get the numbers reduced, which generated a round of applause. In effect, what this officer said was: 'We – like you – really don't want these houses here, but we are forced to accept them by a higher authority.'

Analysis
This scepticism about the project is often seen as downright opposition by the promoters. However, it gives a line of authenticity, which cannot be given by the promoter.

■ *Scepticism.* In addition, it is almost more helpful if they seem 'reluctant brides' to the scheme.

Unfortunately, however, these independent people tend to find that their diaries are very full when approached to appear at these meetings.

THE ROAD TO DAMASCUS

A major new supermarket had been refused planning permission by a local council. This was a major surprise as it had been recommended by the council officials, and seemed to have broad political backing.

However, the local residents' association had spoken out strongly against it on the usual grounds: it was too big, the roads were too crowded, and so on. These obvious rational reasons are never the real reasons. At the council meeting, where the application was rejected, the chairman of the residents' association attended – as was his right – and spoke out against the development.

After we were called in, some minor but very important modifications were made to the plan, particularly regarding open space and where the new doctor's surgery and associated shopping areas would be located. This meant much to the residents' association. Although they were still not particularly happy about the total scheme, they realised it was not going to go away. They decided not to oppose and this time the chairman sat in the public gallery and did not speak. Naturally, this was noted by the politicians in the council chamber.

Analysis
The application was approved almost unanimously. The lesson is that TPAs need not even speak, their actions can speak volumes. Councillors always look in the public gallery before a meeting – the presence of the chairman was noted and his signal taken.

THIRD PARTY ADVOCATES

If the organisation has done its groundwork well, it will know the community and understand it. It will know those people who have an interest in helping the project succeed. It will endeavour to ensure that these people attend, but that they are also well prepared. This does not mean coaching and furnishing prepared scripts. These sorts of initiatives always leak. In addition, they undermine the TPAs, as then they are seen to be company stooges. What is needed is a conversation to remind them to attend and to offer any assistance they may need.

Particularly strong advocates are those who – like St Paul on the road to Damascus – have had a change of heart on the project.

As regards who should attend from the company, there is flexibility. (What is more important is who should not attend – see next section.) However, turning up mob-handed is wrong. At maximum, there should be only three people for most regular meetings. If the meeting is going to be very large (100 plus), then possibly more are needed, but mostly on the logistics front. There are three important roles.

- *Technical expert*. Someone who knows all about the technical aspects of the project. Ideally, they should be an articulate, friendly and, most important, non-confrontational person. In addition, if they turn engineering and technical gobbledegook into reasonable English, it is a real help. These people are – like hen's teeth – rare. Technical people tend to see black and white solutions and often cannot understand irrationality. They then begin to think the audience is stupid. The audience is very quick to sense this and the meeting quickly gets out of control. People from the company side must be able to listen sympathetically, even when a speaker from the floor is talking total drivel. Then they should try to explain gently and be prepared to back down – without conceding the point – when it is useless to go on. The rule is: when in a hole, stop digging. In general, it is unwise to have two technical experts, even from the same company, as they tend to contradict each other on tiny details. This contradiction may not be overt – often it is in the form of further clarifications. This is especially so when a boss attends a presentation by one of his subordinates. (The great example of this is Mrs Thatcher when one of her ministers, Geoffrey Howe, was making a presentation. She interrupted, saying: 'What Geoffrey means to say is…'.) This gives the impression that the company is divided and damages its credibility. It should be said that keeping the boss away is not always the easiest task.

- *Public relations person*. There should be someone attending who is familiar with the politics and the media. His or her job is to handle these people, often by organising an interview with the technical expert. Sitting in on these interviews is a waste of time and is often counter-productive. If the technical expert says something untoward, what can the PR person do about it? – it cannot be undone. On the negative side, the minder gives the impression to the technical expert that he or she is not trusted and it gives exactly the same impression to the journalist.

- *Organiser*. Even if your organisation is not running the event, it is – as noted earlier – your trial. So you want it to go well. An extra pair of hands to make sure the overhead projector works, to make sure that there is coffee and to tend to last-minute emergencies, is vital. It also leaves the technical expert and the public relations person to get on with their work without worrying about logistics. Whoever is representing the organisation should have a proper (hard cover) notebook with them. This allows him to take questions to which the representative does not have the answer, take details and get back to the person who asked the question. This has a number of advantages.

■ It stops people giving commitments – in the heat of this forum – which they cannot honour. One can say: 'I don't know, but I will find out.' Certainly, this can be criticised. The riposte is: 'But you should know.' However, it is still far less dangerous than making false promises which can be extremely expensive in the long run.

■ It allows full and correct information to be imparted, which can be checked by technical and legal experts as appropriate.

■ It shows that you are taking comments seriously. There is always something powerful about things that are written down.

Of course, it is essential that all the questions taken down in writing are answered, and answered fully and promptly. A mechanism for relaying back the answers should be agreed with the chairman in advance.

WHO SHOULD *NOT* ATTEND PUBLIC MEETINGS
Although no-one seems to relish the thought of them, everyone wants to attend public meetings. The more senior the person within an organisation, the keener they are to have rotten tomatoes thrown at them. There is definitely no place at these meetings for the chief executive or managing director, or indeed, ideally, any director. The reasons for this are:

■ *Decision-making power.* These people all have a vast amount of discretion and power. They can make commitments on the spot. So they are asked: 'Will you guarantee this audience here tonight that you will offer full compensation for any damage your facility may bring?' The chief executive has nowhere to run. There are hundreds of questions like this and there are no good answers to any of them at this senior level. However, more junior staff have better answers. For example: 'I am not in a position – as you well know – to make a commitment like this on behalf of the organisation. However, the company will treat all its stakeholders fairly and I will address your concerns when I return. I will come back to you on this.' This gives ample time to compose a response that does not expose the organisation to claims for millions of pounds.

- *Appeal to a higher court.* In the justice system, one can always appeal to a higher court if one is not satisfied with the results in a lower court. It is the same in controversial issues. However, if one uses a senior person right away, then one is effectively going to the Court of Human Rights in the Hague as a first step. There is no further recourse within the company. In other words, if the CEO fails to win the argument, there is nowhere left to appeal. More junior people can always say: 'We will bring this up at the highest level within our company.'

- *Over-robust defences.* As we noted at the beginning of this chapter, the public meeting is replacing hunting with hounds as the blood sport of choice. Although chief executives tend to be fairly tough people, their skills are seldom ideally suited for a robust public meeting. When attacked they tend to defend robustly and, as everyone knows (especially in the corporate battleground) that attack is the best form of defence, that is what they tend to do. However, the objective of attending a public meeting is not to win a debate. It cannot be so. A public meeting only brings heat – not light. At best, it is a forum for bloodletting. Robust defences by the organisation will only harden already hard views.

- *Dented egos.* Chief executives and chairmen like to think that the world loves them – they have worked hard to get where they are and now they want recognition. It can be very hurtful to them when they find out that they are hated figures. Often, they tend to turn on those who have put them in this difficult position when they are hurt. Fragile egos have no place in the public meeting.

Static exhibition

This is by far the best (of a bad lot) of public consultation mechanisms. Ideally, it should be held over a number of days and all of the parameters listed earlier for its organisation should be followed meticulously:

- it should be held in a convenient location (or sometimes locations)
- it should be held at a convenient time (at least part of a weekend)
- it should be heavily advertised well in advance.

The venue

In general, it is better to have a hall that is far too big than one which is far too small. If people are jammed together they can easily and quickly turn into a mob. It should be very central, have a good throughput of people (a community hall or such like) and have ample parking.

EXHIBITION BOARDS

A number of exhibition boards should be placed around the hall. These should be factual and 'spin free'. Of course they will be accused of being favourable towards the company, so all attempts at gloss must be removed, otherwise those who oppose will have their evidence. Each board (or pair of boards) should tell part of the story. For example, in the location of a chemical plant, boards might address:

- the location – where the plant is situated
- the environment – emissions, controls, and so on
- transport – to and from the plant and the materials to be transported
- emergency procedures; how the community will be informed if there is a problem.

COMMENT BOOKS

There should be a comment book for use by staff, if they have a query that they cannot answer and need to get extra information on in order to be able to write to people. Great care should be taken with this book and it should not be left lying around.

Some exhibitions feature a comment book that is left in a prominent position (for example, beside the door) and is used by the public as they leave (in other static exhibitions, questionnaires are used.) However, the comment books tend to fill with either inanities or obscenities. The results from the questionnaires are meaningless, as those who attend the exhibition are not representative. In addition, they will have to be published, so dragging out the whole procedure.

Duration and times of opening

An exhibition which opens from 10.00 am to 12.00 noon and from 2.00 pm to 4.00 pm from Monday to Wednesday in a dormitory town in which a major project can affect residents is worse than useless: it will be seen as a way of avoiding the public. The exhibition must be held at times when it maximises the chances for everyone to see it. The following would be far better:

Friday 3.00 pm – 9.00 pm
(This can catch a number of audiences: those who are picking up children from the school run, those on their way home from work, those who are going to or from their weekly supermarket shopping. It is also held partly in office hours to allow those who have a professional interest to attend in their own work time.)

Saturday 11.00 am – 6 pm
(Again, this will catch shoppers and it will also attract those who will make a special trip just to see the exhibition.)

Sunday 12.00 noon – 5 pm
(This will be convenient for those coming from church or those returning from a lunchtime drink or meal. It also catches those who go out for an afternoon stroll.)

Certainly, for those who have to man these exhibitions, they are very anti-social hours. Effectively, people will have to give up their weekends. However, there is no way out of this. On the positive side, it says to the community that the organisation has done all in its power to consult and inform as widely and as openly as possible. In addition, these times rarely attract chief executives or managing directors, who are best kept away from these events as noted earlier.

Manning
Again, this will depend on the project and numbers expected, but more rather than less is the rule. Remember that one attendee can tie up one of the manning staff for an hour. Also there will be rushes, where at one moment there is no-one and within five minutes there are 30 people in the room. People also need to take a break, so the lowest number one can use is three. Ideally, there should be up to six.

Demeanour and skills
The added advantage of a static exhibition is that one does not need to have the most senior people to man it. However, people must have enough technical expertise to be able to answer questions openly and honestly. The questions and answer sheet (for media) mentioned in Chapter 12 is ideal and the manning staff should be given it well in advance. Before the exhibition opens, there should be a one- to two-hour training session, which also helps bonding.

Argumentative people have no business manning these events: people will have their own views and it is unlikely that the exhibition will change them dramatically.

Manning staff must not be afraid to say: 'I don't know but I will try to find out for you.' That is where the comment book comes in.

Advantages of static exhibitions
There are a number of advantages which static exhibitions have over other forms of public meetings.

AVOIDING THE MOB EFFECT
Certainly, one can get a number of excited people around one of the exhibition boards, pointing to the deficiencies of the plans. However, you can get only so many people into a confined space.

Second, there is no platform, so there is no focal point. In other words, there is no stock in which the organisation sticks its head for people to throw rotten fruit at it.

DIFFUSION OF 'NOISE'
Those who wish to object will certainly turn up at these events. In fact, often more than 80 per cent will be there to protest. However, the protest is diffused over a number of days and many hours. Even the most dedicated protestors get worn down by the sheer time-scales involved: these are long weekends.

Often, one will find a well-publicised protest on the first day with those organisations or people who oppose with placards outside the hall. This is fine and potentially positive, in that it can tend to embarrass those who wish to attend to be informed. Certainly, politicians are not particularly keen on these tactics. Often, the protestors will hand out leaflets and shout out to people as they walk past. Again, this can be counter-productive. No-one likes passing a picket line and that is (in effect) what one is accused of doing, although it is probably not the intention of those in the protest line.

Generally, these dissipate after an hour or so, often when the local newspaper reporter and photographer have been and gone.

IMPARTING REAL INFORMATION
In one-to-one conversations and meetings with individual members of the public, it is possible to have a reasoned debate. As noted above, the objective is not to win this debate, but to impart information. And information can be imparted, assurances can be given in the quiet environment of these exhibitions. People also see real people on the same level: not a spokesman on a platform. This is very powerful. It also allows the more reticent members of the public to have their individual questions addressed.

Static exhibitions – unmanned

Normally, these are held in a public hall and consist of a number of exhibition boards. Sometimes, these are left for a number of days unmanned (for example, in a local library), but in really contentious issues this is unsatisfactory for a number of reasons:

▪ The organisation looks like it is afraid to face its public and is hiding. If it is hiding, it must have done something wrong.

▪ They can never tell the full story, neither can they answer all – or even most – questions. There will always be questions (often highly irrational ones) which the exhibition has not addressed.

▪ As the exhibition boards have to convey the full message, they have to contain a large number of words. People tend either not to read them or to skim them. Others read parts out of context and gain the wrong impression.

▪ Sometimes, a comments book is left with these exhibitions, but they are of little use as many of those who comment refuse (rightly) to leave their names in a public place. However, this is not real feedback.

▪ They are seen as company propaganda – attempting to present a company spin.

▪ They can be defaced and probably will be, so, in very difficult projects, they have little value.

Liaison committees

These are committees where an organisation and an affected community find a forum in which to debate a contentious project – either as one-off meetings or as an ongoing relationship.

There are a number of key factors for success:

1. *Representative.* Given that the majority of people will not attend these meetings and will see attendance as the role of the democratically elected representatives, it is important that these representatives are fully signed up to the process and take an active part in it. Otherwise, one is back to second-guessing the democratic process (see Chapter 12).

2. *Independent.* If the liaison committee is seen as the tame poodle of the organisation, it will surely fail. This is not a propaganda exercise: it is the place where real information is exchanged. Therefore, the chairman

and secretary should come from the community. Certainly, the company may offer assistance in terms of administrative back-up, but the power of the committee should rest with the community. This may sound dangerous. It is no more dangerous than a supermarket leaving goods on its shelves for the public to put in baskets. In fact, this self-regulation can work to the company's advantage: there is often an over-compensation in order to be meticulously fair.

3. *Regular.* If the meetings are held only once a year, one is back to a situation where they are in fact the same as one-off public meetings. There is no continuity; there is no chance for regular exchange of information and pressing issues cannot be put on the back burner for up to 12 months. Anything less than once every three months is too long and shows a lack of commitment by the organisation.

4. *Terms of reference.* These must be formulated jointly with the community and, more important, its representatives and their officials. If these are imposed, they will be resisted and the committee will never work properly. This includes who chairs the committee, who takes minutes, who may speak, and so on.

Of course, all of this is rather frightening after what was said earlier in this chapter about public meetings. Rather than a one-off, it is now to be a regular event. However, it is amazing how quickly the committee settles into its work. Often, the first meeting is like a typical public meeting, with antagonistic questions, heckling and the like. But if the community is genuine about wanting liaison, then it will realise that there is no future in this. That is why it is also so important to have the elected representatives on board. In addition, those in the community who want genuine liaison will tend to shout down those who just want to make noise – the meeting will take on its own positive dynamic.

One of the most successful and long-standing liaison committees is run for the Sellafield nuclear plant.

Naturally, the green groups hate these liaison committees. For a start, as they are run by local representatives, it allows them little chance to bypass the democratic system. Second, if they resort to spoiling tactics, the community turns against them as it is *their* committee. Finally, when companies behave properly and liaise properly these groups have no real function – which, of course, they will not admit.

The liaison committee – as well as its formal business – also offers an occasion for social interaction before and after the meeting. It is a good place to have a quiet word with someone, to run something new past someone else.

In addition, it brings all liaison into a formal setting under one roof with all the key players in the room together. It is a great place to get business done.

THE SELLAFIELD LOCAL LIAISON COMMITTEE

The Sellafield Local Liaison Committee (SLLC) is confined geographically to an area near the nuclear plant in the North West of England. Its terms of reference are: 'The objectives of the committee shall be to serve as a channel of information and comment on those aspects of current and future operations of Sellafield and Drigg sites which may affect the local community or environment; and to satisfy itself that effective plans are maintained for action to be taken in the event of a district hazard arising in the course of the operations and that suitable arrangements are in readiness for implementation of these plans in an emergency.'

There is a wide-ranging cross-section of representation within the 48 members, with many diverse groups represented, from the county, borough and parish councils to the fire service, trades councils, health council, the National Farmers' Union and the local police force. The group is run under the guidelines of an agreed constitution. Members are officially elected to committees and there are strict guidelines governing the chairmanship and vice-chairmanship in relation to BNFL employees, thus encouraging the other members to take the leading role. In fact, BNFL has indicated that it would not accept nomination of the chairmanship of the committee, unless the committee wishes it to do so. The committee meets regularly and the meeting takes place somewhere outside Sellafield itself.

Cllr Bill Minto, leader of Cumbria County Council, has been chairman of the SLLC. He said that the committee had brought 'an increase in the confidence of local people in Sellafield and its activities. The SLLC has provided access and involvement for the man in the street. It serves local democracy in giving the electorate – through their elected representatives – a say in the way Sellafield is run.'

Setting up a liaison committee

It is not particularly important where the initiative to start a liaison committee comes from: often, it will be from the community and, if so, this is excellent.

However, this again is where the diagnostic (Chapter 7) and the enhancements, which will have come from meeting people (Chapter 9), are so important. From these exercises, one will know the views and attitudes of most of the movers and shakers in the community.

In no way should this be used to stack the committee with soft yes men and women. That is one sure route to failure. As noted earlier, it has to be representative and be seen to be representative of the community. However, the diagnostic does give a good inkling as to the final shape and opinions of the committee. If it looks like being run by those who are totally opposed, then, of course, the company has a say. What the diagnostic and other work allows is being able to make that decision with some degree of confidence.

If the approach is to be made by the company, then it should be made informally – as a form of sounding out – to the most appropriate politician. Again, the diagnostic points the way on this: hard and fast rules are not appropriate and are, in fact, highly dangerous. In one area with a specific project, it may be the local member of parliament, in another it may the chairman of the parish council, and in another, the local vicar. Circumstances and personalities will dictate.

Conclusion

If direct public liaison is undertaken in an ordered fashion, it can impart real information to people; it can reassure them and it can provide an excellent forum for getting real views from people and modifying proposals accordingly. However, if it is a foxhunt, its use is little beyond being seen to consult and inform for the sake of it: a fruitless exercise.

Part V
Environmental Credentials

Establishing and Maintaining Environmental Credentials

There are very few organisations which deliberately go out to damage the environment. Yet the activities of people will lead to environmental detriment. Therefore, companies tend to get highly defensive and see environmental communications as a form of fire fighting. But it need not be – it can be a mechanism to improve the business to the benefit of all its stakeholders.

The benefits of environmental credentials

There is no doubt that green sells. However, there is a caveat: green sells when the price differential is not too big. Unleaded petrol – which it is claimed is greener than leaded – did not take off until consumers were given an incentive, in the form of a price reduction, to use it. It was the same with the environmentally friendly detergent Ecover – which never took off because the price was greater than the regular products.

UNHAPPY IN HIS NAPPY

Malcolm Brown is an inventor who came up with a fantastic environmentally friendly idea – a fully biodegradable nappy. According to the *Sunday Times*, Americans get through 18.5 billion of them a year – the majority, once used, going to landfill. The UK supermarkets refused to stock them because they were 15 per cent dearer and customers put price and efficiency before the environment.

UNHAPPY IN HIS NAPPY *(cont'd)*

Analysis

Consumers are likely to buy products to meet their direct needs – not to save the planet.

However, according to a survey by the charity Business in the Community, '86 per cent of consumers are more likely to buy a product associated with a cause or issue'. According to the same survey, the most important causes to consumers are health, education and the environment.

Today, in the UK, one in ten people belongs to an environmental organisation or charity and women are 'significantly more concerned about the environment' according to a DETR survey. In a 1996/7 survey of attitudes to the environment, 24 per cent of people said they bought products because they were environmentally friendly; 29 per cent bought one product over another because of its environmentally friendly packaging. These were not one-off initiatives, they were purchases made on a regular basis.

Greenness adds a perceptual value, which is not a product improvement. However, this needs to be handled with care. Making false claims will soon have the watchful eye of the green movement – rightly – on the miscreant who dares to bend the truth. But greenwashing – as the environmental groups dub it – is now common.

THE SHELL LEGACY

Shell is a giant Anglo-Dutch conglomerate. It is probably no more environmentally damaging than any other oil and chemicals company. And they take the environment seriously and produce an annual environmental report. In 1997, this outlined the steps the company had taken over the year to minimise its impacts on the environment. The report also looked at the company's efforts on sustainable development, climate change, renewable energy, forestry plantations and measuring social impacts. The tone was laudably modest. In the introduction, the Chairman of the Committee of Managing Directors of Shell said: 'We realise that our decisions need to weigh the sometimes conflicting demands of economic and environmental

THE SHELL LEGACY *(cont'd)*

sustainability, and responsibility to the people involved. We know this is difficult but it is a challenge we will not ignore. Part of the solution is in an open dialogue with all concerned. We ask you to regard this report as one part of that process...'

This was Friends of the Earth's response:

Shell Environment Report Condemned as 'Greenwash'

The publication today by Shell of its report on Health, Safety and the Environment was met with accusations of hypocrisy from Friends of the Earth International (FOEI). The commitment in the report to the principle of sustainable development cannot be taken seriously while Shell continues to oppose action to tackle the biggest environmental threat of all – global climate change.

Shell is a member of the Global Climate Coalition (GCC), a powerful lobbying front for the fossil fuel industry, which is scuppering international agreements on cutting greenhouse gas emissions at key climate talks this year, in an attempt to protect the interests of the fossil fuel sector.

Shell's stated support in the report for 'prudent precautionary measures' to reduce greenhouse gas emissions is in direct contradiction to the position of the GCC, which wants governments to reject such measures until there is absolute certainty about the science of climate change. The GCC claims that such action would be premature and would have serious economic impacts.

Anna Stanford, Climate Change Campaigner at FOEI, said:

'Shell must make its mind up. Either it is committed to sustainable development or it is siding with the fossil fuel lobby to prevent action to stop climate change. If Shell is truly committed to the environment it must terminate its membership of the Global Climate Coalition. Shell's research into renewable energy, such as biomass and photovoltaics, carries little credibility while it lobbies against policies that would enable the full potential for renewable energy to be developed.'

Analysis

If your environmental credentials get damaged, as did Shell's over the Brent Spar and Nigeria affairs, then they are very difficult to refurbish – no matter how much money you throw at them. There is little doubt that Shell's environmental performance is probably better than it has ever been – after all, it is still permanently in the spotlight. The green groups know a wounded animal when they see one and they know how to extract the maximum PR benefit from it.

In his book on the public relations industry, *The Invisible Persuaders*, (Bantam Press, 1999) David Michie notes: 'Greenwashing has so quickly become an integral part of corporate and product marketing that consumers now expect that the products and services they use are environmentally friendly. Greenwashing has become part of the advertising and PR landscape. Thus unleaded petrol, in that cheerful, green-striped pump, is heralded as 'environmentally friendly' fuel, even though it contains more of the carcinogen benzene than leaded fuel, not to mention a host of other pollutants such as carbon monoxide, hydrocarbons and carbon dioxide.'

In the 1980s a car company advertised that its new car would help protect the ozone layer because of reduced carbon emissions. The green groups had a field day. Examples such as this are now rare, as the green groups keep a particularly watchful eye on those they see as soft targets.

On the other side of the coin, the Body Shop was the one that benefited most from Shell's discomfiture. It allied itself – particularly with Greenpeace – on the Nigerian human rights activist Ken Saro-Wiwa – to the extent of funding advertising on behalf of Greenpeace.

The Body Shop is unique in that it has grown without recourse to high levels of advertising – it relies on public relations, through strong linkages into green issues – and has built a powerful brand.

In the book *Brand Spirit*, Pringle and Thompson (Wiley, 1999) say:

Anita Roddick's passionate commitment to the environment and abhorrence of the idea of animal testing gave her cosmetics chain a *raison d'être* beyond the provision of beauty treatments and toiletries, despite their undoubted inventiveness as products. The buyers of Body Shop products were not just purchasing efficacious shampoos, nor were they simply acquiring aspiration fashion and image values through colourful and stylish cosmetics. They were voting with their wallets for an ethical stance.

Indeed, the sub-title of this book is 'How Cause Related Marketing Builds Brands' and today there is no greater cause than the environment. Companies that have sound environmental credentials can attach themselves to one of the great causes of the 21st century – the green consumer.

Establishing green credentials

Almost all commercial activities cause some form of environmental damage. Even something as seemingly innocuous as banking has a detriment in terms of electricity use, water use, transport of employees and so on.

However, some firms have seen that, although they may cause major environmental detriment, they can also benefit from doing it sensitively. The more forward thinking ones use it as a marketing tool.

DO-IT-YOURSELF ENVIRONMENTAL KIT

B&Q is the UK's biggest retailer of do-it-yourself goods. According to the company, 'our most significant impact on the environment is caused by the 40,000 products we sell at B&Q. We are completely committed to reducing that impact.'

'In 1990, B&Q undertook research to identify the environmental issues that needed to be addressed. Specific policies were then devised and individual action plans formulated with targets to be achieved.'

This extensive programme covered seven main areas:

1. *Suppliers.* The company knows that it has the power 'to encourage its 600 suppliers to be committed to improving their environmental performance'. Targets set for 1994 resulted in over 95 per cent of their suppliers producing a meaningful environmental policy and action plan. In 1991 this figure was less than 10 per cent.

2. *Working conditions in developing countries.* Like the Body Shop, B&Q sees a blurring of the lines between environmental and social responsibility. Their approach has been to tackle the issues through partnerships with development agencies across the world. 'We started with the Philippines and India, and in 1998 our work expanded into China. For example, B&Q was the first retailer to stock rugs which come from looms certified by Rugmark as not using illegal or exploited child labour. Rugmark is an independent charity supported by Christian Aid and Oxfam.'

3. *Timber policy and targets.* About 22 per cent of the company's turnover is accounted for by timber, so this was an area where they looked to improve environmental credentials. In 1991, they announced two targets in this area which, by the end of 1995, would ensure that B&Q had identified all its timber sources and that all of its timber products would derive from well-managed forests. The company had a target that, by the end of 1999, it would only purchase timber-based products from forests independently certified by a certifier accredited by the Forest Stewardship Council (FSC). The FSC is a global organisation which has set the principles of good forest management against which forest-specific standards can be measured and can check the quality of the forest certifier's work.

DO-IT-YOURSELF ENVIRONMENTAL KIT *(cont'd)*

4. *Product and packaging disposal.* Here the emphasis is on minimisation which can, of course, also lead to improved profits. For example, in 1996 B&Q decided to remove the tray from its own-label wooden toilet seat. This was made from polystyrene, which is difficult for customers to recycle. A further advantage was that the number of seats which could go into a 40ft container for shipping increased from 3,300 to 4,500, making an overall financial saving of over £100,000 a year and reducing transport pollution.

5. *Paint.* The key environmental impact of paint is the release of VOCs (volatile organic compounds), primarily solvents, into the atmosphere, which contribute to photochemical smog. VOCs also cause the unpleasant smell associated with paint and can be harmful to people, especially asthmatic children.

    The company aimed to reduce the total quantity of VOCs in paint products sold through their stores by 30 per cent by the end of 1999, using 1996 as the baseline. In addition, they are continually working to introduce low VOC products.

6. *Peat.* B&Q does not take peat from SSSIs (sites of special scientific interest) which have a particular conservation value. However, the company recognises that many of their customers still want to use peat products and, although 'actions will be taken to reduce our dependency on peat... these actions will not compromise product performance or customer confidence'. The company stocks a range of alternatives to peat and has peat-based products at competitive prices.

7. *Being a good neighbour.* With almost 300 sites and a major distribution network, B&Q has made a major environmental impact by its very existence. The company recognises the huge potential for reducing waste disposal costs by recycling. For example, it is estimated that by hauling back cardboard, plastics, metals and wooden pallets to a central distribution centre for recycling, there will be a saving of about £500,000 a year.

    B&Q's energy needs generate 115,000 tonnes of carbon dioxide a year. The pattern of energy use of each store is closely monitored and compared with standards. The latest stores are equipped with building management systems which control energy use from a central source. Staff are able to check electricity use, light levels and temperatures, and exert local control as necessary, all via a single touchscreen.

B&Q introduced a Green Grants Scheme whereby stores can apply for up to £250 worth of products to be used for an environmental project in their area. Since the launch of this scheme, 320 grants have been awarded, ranging from school

---

DO-IT-YOURSELF ENVIRONMENTAL KIT *(cont'd)*

wildlife gardens to river clean-ups and building a walkway across a nature reserve. Since April 1998, stores have been encouraged to contact their local authorities to discuss opportunities for partnership.

Analysis

Most of the environmental actions taken by B&Q also make substantial business sense. Many contribute directly to the bottom line. In addition, the company gets an important marketing advantage by its linkage to a powerful cause – the environment. Naturally, the company – through advertising, brochures and public relations – promotes its environmental stance. However, the tone of voice used in these environmental promotions is low-key and modest. There is no bragging and an ongoing admission that more needs to be done.

So how do companies manage, protect and mature their reputation in a green world? Corporate reputations should be built up from the micro-level as B&Q have shown and as the other chapters in this part suggest. To maintain a good reputation a company or group should always be prepared for incidents like that which afflicted Perrier. It is about attention to detail: ensuring you can prove that what you say is true and being ready to admit when you are wrong. You should be aware of your weaknesses before anyone else and act on them. It is the minute detail that will be picked up by the press and, by implication, the public.

However, many companies are intrinsically green. Like B&Q, they too can make a virtue out of reality.

GREEN BLOCKS

Housebuilders are perceived by many to be despoilers of the countryside and are popular targets for many green groups. Companies that make the building materials for these housebuilders are often seen – by association – also to be detrimental to the environment.

Marley Building Materials pioneered a product called Thermalite 50 years ago. These blocks are made using over 50 per cent pulverised fuel ash, which is a waste product from power stations. Thermalite also recycles the majority of waste

GREEN BLOCKS *(cont'd)*

produced during the manufacturing process, and what cannot be recycled is used either in other concrete products or as an aggregate bulk fill replacement in road construction.

As aircrete blocks are lightweight, there are substantial cost savings and subsequent reductions in energy use during haulage. Thermalite is also an excellent insulator, so reducing the need for other – often petroleum-based – insulation products.

Analysis

House buyers – as in all other commercial sectors – will demand products which have green credentials. By promoting these – again in an ethical, honest and low-key way – the company believes that it can gain market advantage over other products. And by giving house builders an extra environmental credential – in the shape of the block from which the house is built – they will also get a market advantage by specifying the Marley product.

Conclusion

The environment is quasi-sacred in the modern Western world and linking a brand to the environment may be advantageous. For products with similar price and quality, an environmentally related aura can only be helpful in the marketplace.

16

Conclusion: Green can be Irrational

In the middle of the 19th century, a Catholic monk started interfering with nature. By 1865, Gregor Johann Mendel had published his 'laws' following his experiments of inbreeding lines of pea plants by means of repeated self-pollination. This gross interference with the natural law caused no outrage, no indignation, nothing. In fact, it was not until 1900 that three other botanists stumbled across Mendel's work and realised its significance. Today, this pioneering work is at heart of modern agriculture. We all eat modified food – especially vegetarians.

If we move forward a century and imagine that Mendel's work had lain undiscovered and was only found in the year 2000, would we accept it as we do now? Of course not. There would the same outrage that has greeted GM crops.

Science moves on and new techniques are discovered. But there is uproar. In the mid-1990s, the release of these GM foods had governments, European institutions and the media in a lather. Even an august broadcasting body such as the BBC referred to 'Frankenstein foods' – the handy label applied by the green groups. If the green groups and the media had been about in 1900, no doubt Mendel's work would have been greeted in the same way.

The world of environmental issues management is certainly a very tough one. To win the arguments, those who advocate progress will have to enter into this fray much more than they have done in the past. Not just by fighting the battle on rational grounds – unsuccessfully, as did Brent Spar and Monsanto – but by entering into the debate on the emotional as well as the rational front. But these people cannot work alone. They need advocates for their causes.

To scientists and engineers, this emotional irrational side may seem to be irrelevant and they are often seen as seeking to trivialise serious issues.

This is often the case when a company decides to promote its environmental credentials – the scheme is derided as a stunt. However, for those who are high upon Maslow's hierarchy, the trivial is very important.

Part of the reason for the rise in environmental consciousness in the developed world is the problem of overpopulation: we are living on top of each other. And while population in these countries is relatively slow growing, people are turning to the cause of 'protecting the environment' as a façade for jealously protecting their own comfortable life-style. In addition, we have to square our own irrationality. It should be very difficult to say 'I do not believe in cars' if you drive one, or 'I don't believe there should be any more houses' if you live in one. But that is exactly what happens as this case shows.

THE OPPOSITION TO HOUSING

Southern England is one of the most congested parts of Europe. There are 30 million people crammed into a tiny area around London. They are affluent, they have houses, they have cars, they have a life-style and now they have a huge environmental consciousness and consciences. The demand for housing will continue to rise – about four million units by 2011, according to government statistics. This is because of the need to replace the existing housing stock, more people living alone after divorce, people living longer, people keeping two homes, and so on.

However, there is a major backlash against the building of new houses in the South of England, particularly those which are to be built on 'green fields' – land which has only been used for agriculture or the like. Why? After all, we all (except for the environmentalists who mount tree protests and the homeless) live in houses. And without doubt the site of our house was once a green field at some stage.

Ask anyone if they are concerned about the homeless and the answer will almost certainly be 'yes'. Ask if they should be housed, and again the answer is 'yes'. But there is a total contradiction here. If no more new houses are built, there can be only one consequence as the economic laws of supply and demand predict – the price of housing will go up. The rich are safe – the difference between £5 million and £7 million for a mansion is immaterial.

The middle classes will struggle on making sacrifices – after all, the Englishman's home is his castle. The lower middle classes will begin to rely on government, but more and more of the very poorest will fall off the ladder and the inevitable result is an increase in homelessness.

THE OPPOSITION TO HOUSING *(cont'd)*

Analysis

Yet people continue to oppose new house building, despite the fact that they do not want more homeless people. The concept of NIMBY has moved to BANANA (build absolutely nothing anywhere near anyone). But this now has a respectable new façade – the selfishness of NIMBYism has moved to the acceptable face of protecting the environment. Arguments like: 'The reason we don't want houses here is that it is a historic site/birds live here/it will ruin the landscape' and so on are trotted out. One of the real reasons, a fear that it will damage house prices, is never mentioned.

And the irrationality continues into the campaigning groups. The Council for the Protection of Rural England (CPRE) recruits many of its members from the landed gentry, some of whom live in very big houses indeed. Surely, if they are against further development, the one obvious solution is to let the spare rooms in their houses to the less well-off. One cannot see this finding much favour.

Their arguments are about protecting the countryside for future generations: obviously, one way would be to demolish some of the existing houses – usually inhabited by the wealthy (perhaps CPRE members) – often in specially designated areas of outstanding natural beauty, and return the site to nature.

So why is it that advances – which might have some environmental impact – are seen as 'bad' when scientists (and often governments, as in the case of genetically modified foods) see them as 'good'? Is it the media who are only too quick to pick on every scare story imaginable? Is it the green groups, who are only too happy to feed the media? Or are we seeing the rise of a modern pantheism, where the environment is the new god, replacing the old god of organised religion? Today, the great sins are the felling of a tree or the building of a house.

But as noted earlier, the objection to the building of a house is irrational if you live in one – as most of us do. Often, these irrational objections are countered with rational arguments. This is absolutely futile. The irrational must be countered with the irrational. Yet organisations have great problems with this. But why? Marketing is based on the irrational. To gain acceptance, science will have to market itself and its advances much in the same way as Papa and Nicole sell the Renault Clio. Does anyone know what a Clio engine looks like?

Unlike the laws of nature, the laws of man are irrational. Just because something is logical or even true does not mean that it is acceptable. Even our system of government is acknowledged to be flawed: 'Democracy substitutes election by the incompetent many for appointment by the corrupt few,' as George Bernard Shaw put it so eloquently. Politicians know this only too well. Tony Blair's spin doctors bleep him when his hair has blown out of place. What has a man's hair got to do with the ability to run a country, one asks. In a democracy, irrationality rules through the 'incompetent many'.

And, every individual has individual opinions. In a democracy perfect agreement on everything is not possible. The best that can be hoped for is agreement on some issues. So the political parties are broad churches. They allow for a variety of views to exist within an overall umbrella of agreement.

Finally, the fears of the irrational cannot be countered with logical arguments. A key to this is the law of the absolute. For example, to the question: 'Can you guarantee that this product will never cause any damage to anyone?' there is no meaningful answer. It is this absolutist argument that lost the BSE (mad cow disease) argument, the Brent Spar and now GM foods as well as many other arguments. People may say that the chance of getting CJD (the human equivalent of BSE), are substantially less than the risks of death from smoking a cigarette. It's immaterial. The logical argument does not stand up. In banning beef on the bone, Jack Cunningham, then the UK Agriculture Minister, made a decision based on irrational emotions because he is a rational politician.

But in this new millennium, overpopulation in a developed country is felt harder than ever thanks to the car. Personal mobility and freedom is a second nature to mankind. When pre-historic man first saw a horse, it was love. It meant freedom to travel. People love to use their cars: the government which tries to tinker with this symbol of independence and freedom is not going to be popular. But the roads are heavily congested. People have seen that more houses mean more cars. It is not uncommon for a family of four with two grown-up children living at home to have four cars. The cost of entry is very low: for under £1,000 you can be on the road.

So the cry goes out: 'Stop development – it causes pollution' (environmental consciousness) – 'more people will mean more cars which means it will be more difficult for me to get around in comfort' (the real reason). Yet people react against rises in the cost of fuel and road taxes – all measured and designed to reduce car use – because these limit their ability to enjoy *their* cars. People do not want to give up their cars, they want other people to give up theirs.

Today, the selfish face of NIMBYism is masked by the honourable façade of protecting the environment.

Conclusion

This book could be seen to present a pretty sad view of the world. A world where all progress grinds to a halt because the rich decide that they have moved – in the words of the strapline of the environmental newspaper *Planet on Sunday* – 'Towards heaven on Earth.' Are we reaching the end of the Renaissance of science and technology that began about 1500, and are we about to enter into another Dark Age, where all progress is seen as bad?

To maintain progress so that our grandchildren can have the start in life that our grandparents left us is going to take brave people. To try to ensure that that inheritance is more equally spread among all the citizens of the planet – not just the cosseted few in the environmentally aware developed world – is going to take very brave people indeed.

And those who take this approach in environmentally sensitive projects will be successful and will thrive. In marketing today, one of the newer, more successful tools is cause-related marketing, where a company or brand is linked to a cause or issue.

And the greatest cause of today – is the environment. For companies that can manage their environmental credentials well – and that means with modesty and honesty – the environment is the ultimate marketing cause.

Of course, progress cannot simply come to a grinding halt. 1957 was designated International Geophysical Year, and it seemed then that science and technology would offer a global panacea. That dream was exaggerated, but it should not be forgotten that much has been delivered as we now know, but the sentiment expressed at that time by Dr Odish, the Executive Director for US National Committee, went like this:

> Provided that the complexity of modern society does not hide what is at hand, provided that the destructive forces present in our day not only do not eliminate civilisation but do not, by their necessary insistence upon man's attention, mask the wonders of earth and universe, and provided that teachers and poets, scientists and philosophers sense the possibilities, there is at hand an unparalleled situation for stimulating the best in man.

It is still true today.

Index